REAL MANAGERS REVISITED

ISBN: 978-0-578-43652-4

For information, contact Hogan Press
11 S. Greenwood, Tulsa OK 74120
hoganassessments.com

HOGANPRESS

Interior Book Design by
Michelle M. White

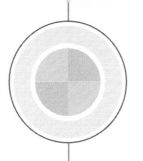

Real
Managers
Revisited

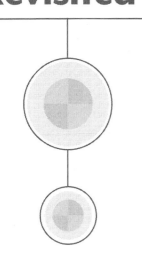

Luthans

Hodgetts

Rosenkrantz

Ashton

Table of Contents

Robert Hogan's *PREQUEL to*
REAL MANAGERS REVISTED

FRED LUTHANS AND COLLEAGUES' BOOK, *REAL MANAGERS,* is a milestone contribution to management research. The size of his sample, the duration of his study, the variety of measures he used, and his robust conclusions suggest the book should be a citation classic. Alas, the book seems to be "more honored in the breach than the observance"; put differently, modern management consultants and researchers seem to have ignored the book. The purpose of this revisitation of Luthans and colleagues' classic is to redirect attention to the importance of this research and its conclusions.

Given the fact that Luthans's research is so good, why has the book been ignored? Besides being caught up in publisher problems, one reason is that management research, like popular music, is subject to fads, and Luthans's book was never associated with popular fads such as "agile leadership" or "transformational leadership". A second reason, I suspect, is that that leadership researchers, management consultants, and executive recruiters didn't like his message. Actually, there are two messages. The first is that organizations like, reward, and promote managers who stand out and make a strong positive impression—whether or not they demonstrate any talent for management. People who are charismatic and stand out seem leaderlike and therefore attract the attention of key decision makers. Luthans suggests that everyone is wrong. Modern research shows that charisma is correlated with narcissism and that narcissistic managers are incompetent leaders: they make overly aggressive and risky decisions, they won't solicit advice, and they won't listen to feedback.

The second message is that organizations tend to ignore or pass over managers who are good at their primary task—building effective teams. Unfortunately, these team-builders may be unable to make a strong impression. Leadership is not about finding a way into the spotlight, leadership is about building and maintaining high performing teams. So, the big message of Luthans's book is that organizations tend to promote into leadership positions people who may or may not have any talent for leadership.

Luthans's message is corroborated by Collins's justly famous book *Good to Great*. The book concerns the determinants of organizational effectiveness. The book concludes that the key factor driving the performance of highly successful organizations is the leadership provided by the CEO. And the CEOs of highly successful organizations share two important characteristics. First, they are unusually persistent and tenacious in the pursuit of success. And second, they are quiet, understated, and humble. Which means these effective CEOs would likely have been overlooked in many organizations because they didn't stand out.

An emerging theme in leadership research shows that humility is associated with effective leadership; unlike narcissists, humble leaders are willing to solicit input, acknowledge their mistakes, and make corrections. But most importantly, humility is the opposite of narcissism and narcissistic leaders are toxic. Luthans's book reported the first major study to point out that organizations often promote people into leadership positions using the wrong criteria. This message seems to still hold true today and continues to serve as a strong empirical backdrop for *Real Managers Revisited.*

Preface to the Revisitation

THIS BOOK IS ABOUT MANAGERS IN THE REAL WORLD. These managers—Real Managers, or RMs, as we call them—are not the visible, charismatic leaders of industrial giants or even the highly successful executives from so-called excellent firms. They are not the managers described in best-selling management tomes. Instead, they are mainstream managers from middle-of-the-road organizations. They are the great mass of managers who get things done every day in organizations large and small, national and local, famous and obscure. Our book was the first to make an empirical investigation of what RMs really do in their day-to-day activities, and to dig deep into how the successful and effective ones do things differently from their unsuccessful and less effective counterparts. In short, this book is about Real Managers in real organizations, managers with titles such as plant manager, department head, store manager, agency chief, or district manager, from organizations of all sizes in both the private and public sectors.

We gathered data from 457 RMs from numerous organizations in a massive four-year study using multiple methods. We built the empirical database for the book from the free observation of 44 RMs in order to determine their managerial activities. Then, trained participant observers systematically gathered data on 248 other RMs in their natural settings. In addition to the free and systematic observation data, we also collected standardized questionnaire data from the RMs' subordinates, and data from intensive interviews of 165 RMs. Chapter Two goes into the details of this study, which was the first of its kind.

We wrote this book for you—the professional manager. As such, it highlights the real-life experiences of RMs as much as possible. In this revisitation, we have included a new introduction by renowned psychologist Robert Hogan, bringing the book's conclusions forward into the 21st century and the economy of the Third Industrial Revolution. In addition, we have reorganized the original text to emphasize the real-life experiences of RMs even more. We continue to feel that the empirical backdrop of the book is a major strength, and a real difference from the popular business books so familiar to managers. Therefore, we have decided to present some of the methods and numerical analysis used in our quantitative study in a separate chapter (the aforementioned Chapter Two). As a rule of thumb, we wrote for the professional manager, the Real Manager that this book studies. We hope that our academic colleagues, interested in such things as reliability coefficients and statistical significance tests, will continue to find enough satisfying detail and will use the extended reference section at the end of the book to pursue any unanswered questions or desires for more details on the study.

The study that formed the basis for the book had three major phases. In the first phase, we attempted to find an answer to the seemingly obvious, yet intriguing question, *What do managers really do?* We used the findings in the first phase of our work as a point of departure for the more difficult second and third phases. In the second phase, our question was more specific: *What do **successful** managers really do?* In the third and final phase, we tried to answer perhaps the most important question: *What do **effective** managers really do?* Using these three questions as a conceptual framework, we attempt to find answers for RMs throughout the book.

In the late 1980s, there was considerable interest in and concern about American business and managers. Once foreign competition, declining productivity, increasing costs, decreasing profits and service, and disgruntled employees finally received the attention of managers across the country, they turned for answers to best-selling books to see how Lee Iacocca managed Chrysler, Harold Geneen managed ITT, and the executives in Peters and Waterman's "excellent" firms did things. Practicing managers obviously found these accounts interesting reading, and, along with Blanchard and Johnson's "one-minute" solutions, they got some good ideas and specific techniques. But after that first wave of attention, we felt it was time to flesh out what was really going on in mainstream organizations and what RMs, especially successful and effective ones, were doing in these organizations.

Our book starts from square one. It makes no assumptions about what managers *should* be doing in terms of the traditional prescriptions, or *could* be doing if they had been in Lee Iacocca's shoes or worked for one of Peters and Waterman's "excellent" companies. It also makes no assumptions about fundamental changes in the quarter century since it was first written. RMs continue to wrestle with the day-to-day and face-to-face challenges of management that they did in the '80s and '90s. Instead, thanks to our intensive empirical investigation of what RMs do and what the successful and effective ones do differently than their unsuccessful and less effective counterparts, we dissipate myths about how practitioners *should* manage to be successful and effective. After all, we went to the best source possible for learning how to be successful and effective: Real Managers in real organizations, instead of professors, consultants, writers, or CEOs of glamourous companies.

In particular, this book attempts to replace the myths about the nature of managerial work and how to be successful and effective at it with data-based, systematic analysis. Even more, we explore what the relationship is between managerial success and managerial effectiveness. Almost all management writing uses the terms "successful" and "effective" interchangeably; in fact, one of the dominant myths surrounding the field of management is that successful managers are the same as effective managers. We buy neither the argument nor the mythic conclusion. In the real world, success and effectiveness are decidedly *not* the same thing. If RMs are successful, in the sense of being rapidly promoted and/or being the heads of their respective organizations, does that mean they are effective? Our answer is no, and the implications of this will become disturbingly clear as the chapters unfold.

We give specific treatment to the major findings from our investigation of RM activities in separate chapters. We examine traditional management (Chapter Five), communication (Chapter Six), networking (Chapter Seven), and human resource management (Chapter Eight)—all of which emerged as particularly important activities of RMs. We were generally impressed with the RMs we studied, and we demonstrated that they can learn from one another. They didn't have to turn to the Japanese or Lee Iacocca or the executives in the excellent companies two decades ago, and they don't have to mimic the latest management fads today, to manage effectively. The major lesson to be learned from this book is that the ways to be successful and effective can be found in Real Managers themselves.

Because of the size and length of the study upon which this book is based, there were many people who made important contributions along the way. In particular, we would like to recognize and thank Professor Diane Lee Lockwood for her many ideas and considerable work on the first phase of the study. Also, we would like to acknowledge and thank Professors Avis Johnson and Harry Hennessey for being part of the research team during the middle phases of the study, and Lew Taylor in the later phases. We would also like to acknowledge the great administrative support we have received from Wendy Howell in making this revisitation a reality, including discovering our talented, knowledgeable new co-author James Ashton. Finally, we would like to especially thank Dr. Hogan, not only for writing the Prequel to frame the book for today's RMs, but for believing our original findings had lasting insights and still-valuable lessons for modern managers. From the beginning, *Real Managers* aimed to restore the confidence of American managers in themselves, and it continues to do so in this revisitation.

Fred Luthans, Richard M. Hodgetts,
Stuart A. Rosenkrantz, and James Ashton

CHAPTER **ONE**
Real Managers in the Real World

MANAGEMENT BOOKS ARE FLOODING THE MARKET. MOST of them paint a seductive portrait: the promise that *this* one will reveal the hidden secrets to effective management. This manager's El Dorado or Shangri-la contains the keys that will enable managers to climb the ladder of success in their organization, all the while effectively leading their people and operations. For the most part, it's a pipe dream. *Real Managers* also wants to put managers on the road to success and effectiveness, but unlike all the others, our book is based on empirical data about Real Managers in real organizations. Using participant direct observation data, supplemented by interviews and questionnaires, we asked what Real Managers do in their day-to-day activities, what Real Managers who have been successful in being rapidly promoted in their organizations do, and finally, what Real Managers who are effective in managing their people and operations do.

These three seemingly simple questions had surprisingly different answers. That is, Real Managers in the aggregate acted differently from those who experienced relatively rapid promotions in their organizations (we call them *successful* Real Managers) and those whose subordinates had relatively high satisfaction and commitment and were judged to have effective organizational units (we call them *effective* Real Managers). We should pause here to emphasize our definition. Successful Real Managers get promoted quickly; effective Real Managers lead satisfied teams and organizational units that contribute to the bottom line.

Even more important, we observed that successful RMs *behaved* quite differently than effective RMs. This finding has profound implications, and may begin to explain the cause of many of the problems currently facing American organizations. Could it be that the wrong people are being promoted? Could it be that the managers who are effective with their people and their unit's performance are not the ones on the fast track? These intriguing questions, and the evidence-based answers to them, form the basis of our inquiry.

This book, then, presents Real Managers—RMs—in their everyday, often mundane, sometimes stressful, work lives. On one hand, this is an ambitious undertaking, for RMs do many different things. On the other hand, their activities can fit into an overall framework that allows systematic analysis and evaluation. How RMs have traditionally been portrayed in business literature and popular media may be accurate in the overall parameters, but this picture still contains much pure conjecture or inference based on a desire to fill in the missing links. In retrospect, there have probably been more myths regarding RMs than there have been facts. Nearly all popular management books and college textbooks to date are prescriptive: they relate what managers *should* do. This book, in contrast, is based on an empirically based description of what they *really* do, and what that implies.

Most of us would agree that managers rely on their colleagues and coworkers—they get things done through people—but how precisely does this happen? Is it a formal process that is preplanned and effectively executed? Or is it a free-flowing type of process that involves a great deal of helter-skelter activity? Tradition says management is, or at least should be, a rational process. After all, modern management was born when people in the big industries of the Second Industrial Revolution started thinking they could apply scientific rigor to business; thus "scientific management." Much more recently, a small but influential view is that RMs race through their work, often spending no more than a few minutes on each of their varied activities. Management professionals and academics have been constructing theories about management for decades, even centuries. But in this book, we instead go to the source by reporting what we learned from actual observation of RMs in their natural settings. As the chapters unfold, we will lay out a detailed description of what Real Managers do, what successful Real Managers do, and what effective Real Managers do.

Recall our separate definitions of successful RMs versus effective RMs. You might be wondering why we keep harping on this, because you're used to those two words meaning about the same thing. The truth is that success and effectiveness are very different attributes, and we make a clear distinction between them, even though these two terms are used interchangeably in management literature and by most of us in our everyday language. This crucial difference is tied to and confirmed by our rigorous empirical analysis of RMs, and it constitutes one of our key themes. Because we needed an operational, measurable definition of success and of effectiveness, we developed specific and detailed measurement indices for each. We will describe these indices more fully in the next chapter; for now, we simply want to make a clear, measured distinction between successful RMs and effective RMs. The significance of this distinction will become clear as the book unfolds.

Besides making the distinctions between myth and reality and between successful and effective, this book illustrates the relationship between theory and practice. Management theory tries to explain why managers act the way they do; management practice describes what managers do. The two approaches, theory and practice, have important but generally ignored linkages.

Our story of Real Managers starts with the distinction between management myth and reality: the difference between what managers tend to believe about their work based on management literature, and the reality of what our extensive study shows RMs doing in the real world. Then we turn to the study itself. Because it was the first of its kind, we feel it is important to outline the study in some detail, to set the context for what follows. After identifying the key components of the study, we get to the heart of the matter by detailing RMs' activities: what they do and why they do it. The middle part of the book (Chapters Five through Eight, on traditional management activities, communication, networking, and human resource management) exposes the whys and wherefores of RMs. These chapters weave our empirical findings into existing theory and the actual practice of RMs.

Chapter Nine comes full circle, providing closure for our study of RMs and integrating and sorting out what we found. In addition, we analyze the fit between our findings and existing management theory and practice. Finally, we ask one last key question: what do Real Managers who are both successful *and* effective do? You, dear reader, as a Real Manager on the front lines of today's organizational battlefields, surely want to know how to best combine these two desired outcomes. We therefore conclude by identifying managerial skills needed now and in the future to become an effective *and* successful Real Manager.

CHAPTER **TWO**
Myth and Reality in the Management Jungle

We all went through the b-schools when we were young, and the professors had all the answers on the blackboards, computer printouts, and reading assignments. Everything was so clean and precise. The problems in the accounting and quantitative courses always had logical answers. Even the principles of management and policy courses had structure and form, citing the five functions a manager performs, or the three steps of strategic planning. The same is true of the management development programs I have attended over the years. The trainer has all the answers to my problems—one, two, three. But I'm here to tell you it really isn't like that. My day consists of running from one meeting to the next, fielding questions from my internal staff and outsiders, trying to respond to telephone messages, trying to smooth over an argument between a couple of people, and keeping my ever higher in-basket from toppling down on top of me. In fact, I feel guilty that I'm not doing the things that the management educators, trainers, and the things I read say that I should be doing. When I come out of one of these sessions, or after reading the latest management treatise, I'm eager and ready to do it. Then the first phone call from an irate customer, or a new project with a rush deadline, falls on me, and I'm back in the same old rut. I don't have time for time management, let alone strategic planning and designing a matrix structure for my unit.

THERE IS A STARK DIFFERENCE BETWEEN MOST OF THE normative prescriptions for managers and how Real Managers act in real life. Many of the myths surrounding the nature of managerial work have been challenged only recently. We found that when our Real Managers were unobtrusively observed in their natural, day-to-day work situations, they behaved quite differently than the ways that popular airport-management books, textbooks, periodicals, common opinion, or even sophisticated research (depending mainly on questionnaire data and very confusing statistical analysis and conclusions) have described over the years. This discrepancy, between traditional beliefs about what managers do and what Real Managers were observed to do, strains the credibility of much that has been written about managers and management. We want to explode some of the common myths about management, and contrast them with reality.

The discrepancy between commonly held beliefs and expectations about what managers *should* be doing, what academics *think* they're doing, and what they *really* do was disturbing even to some of the Real Managers themselves, as the RM whose words opened this chapter graphically illustrated. Real Managers have been faced with this dilemma for years. They say to themselves, "The article/book/professor/trainer says one thing, but I'm doing something else. I must be wrong, because what I'm doing has little or nothing to do with what they are talking about." What the articles, books, professors, and trainers are talking about may be just myths surrounding the nature of managerial work. What are these myths? Let's dig into them in detail.

MYTH NO. 1:
Managers Do Reflective, Strategic Planning

Traditional management theory says that all managers systematically receive information that enables them to anticipate future developments in time to adapt to expected needs in some orderly manner. In other words, they do reflective, strategic planning. We found that Real Managers do some planning (see Figure 2-2), but not necessarily in the sophisticated ways portrayed in the strategic management literature. More realistically, higher-level managers proceed with caution and plain old-fashioned fear, both natural and appropriate reactions, when making decisions. This process is not what the textbooks describe as strategic planning, but the practical result is in some ways similar. Decisions are deferred or delayed until as much information as possible is gathered at the higher levels. Unfortunately, however, the more time taken for decision-making at the top, the less time is available for mid- and lower-level managers to plan and execute. This makes the RMs' jobs more chaotic and it limits their planning to a reactive, short-run (or even immediate), tactical approach, rather than a reflective, strategic approach.

MYTH NO. 2:

Managers Organize Work Through Formal Structures and Procedures

Managers are commonly believed to organize by designing formal authority/responsibility structures. Yet in real organizations, higher-ups are liable to discourage or even prohibit managers from formalizing all structures and procedures. As they see it, in most organizations paper is already the "most important product." As shown in Figure 2-2, we found paperwork to be one of the most dominant activities of Real Managers. More importantly, however, we also discovered that Real Managers deliberately avoid paperwork, which goes hand-in-hand with formalized structures and the accompanying written policies and procedures. Additionally, top-level centralized control aborts any attempt by mid- or lower-level managers to implement their own authority/responsibility structures. Instead, managers more often organize their teams through meetings and on the basis of personality and style (i.e., the networking activity of RMs), rather than through formalized structures and procedures.

MYTH NO. 3:

Managers Do Systematic, Proactive Staffing

Traditionally, managers staff by anticipating and planning proactively for future personnel and training needs in their area of responsibility. Then they select, train, and evaluate their people—that is, they perform a proactive staffing function. As Figure 2-2 shows, Real Managers do relatively little of this staffing activity. We found that unless RMs were part of long-range planning to create or to phase down their operations, they had little warning of future staffing needs. More often than not, their people left on very short notice, due to accidents, health, or personal reasons. One manager explained:

> *This notion of proactive human resource planning is ridiculous. Over the 13 years I have been in charge of this department, I have had my share of turnover, but very little of it I could anticipate or plan for. Sure, I know about contingency planning and probability estimates. But I still maintain that it makes no sense in predicting*

who quits and who doesn't, or how many will quit in a
given period of time. I just have to react to the personal
whims of my people as they come and go.

Very few organizations maintain a pipeline of suitable hiring candidates. Typical search periods of two to 20 weeks, or even longer, are not uncommon when trying to replace employees. Real Managers have to face this problem constantly; the training/developing aspect of human resource management becomes an eternal struggle to survive, with the immediate goal of simply maintaining current productivity—let alone improving it. The appraisal aspect of the staffing function becomes a bureaucratic requirement to fill out some subjective forms once or twice a year.

MYTH NO. 4:
Managers Operate Under Well-Defined Chains of Command

Traditional management assumes that unity of command prevails; each manager reports to only one boss in the chain of command. Yet, as one manager described, this assumption may not be valid:

> *During the course of a single day, I am interrupted and*
> *diverted from what I'm doing on an almost continual*
> *basis. When I plan my day, the list of to-dos helps keep*
> *me from getting lost among the interruptions. But I'm a*
> *results-oriented manager, and it's frustrating to see the*
> *amount of work that I'm not getting done. Upper-level*
> *management acts as if they're still operating at my level.*
> *Why can't they grow into the level to which they've been*
> *promoted? I've counted at least a dozen people who tell*
> *me to drop whatever I'm doing to go to an unscheduled*
> *meeting, or to do something I don't want to do or really*
> shouldn't *do, in order to do my job properly.*

The managers making peremptory demands on others sincerely believe that their requirements are a justifiable exception in the chain of command. Here again, we found that Real Managers are coping creatively with a problem that traditional theory tells us should not exist.

MYTH NO. 5:

Traditional Principles Simplify Managing

There is a kind of holy writ of management. For every possible management situation, a traditional management principle exists to tell RMs what they *should* do. These traditional principles, designed to simplify the managerial process, may be delivering less than promised. Although we definitely found RMs doing them (see Figures 2-2 and 2-3), these principles can be confusing at best and contradictory at worst. Their greatest contribution may be simply to provide us with a common managerial vocabulary, but as we examined them in detail, the imperfections became painfully clear. A review of some of these principles will point out the difficulty, if not the impossibility, that RMs face in reconciling them in any given situation.

The pioneering management theorist Henri Fayol identified five functions of management: planning, organizing, commanding, coordinating, and controlling. Management texts still teach these five functions, in one form or another, and beginning management students are duly impressed. "Here are the five things that you, as a manager, must do to win the game—to be effective," the texts declare. No wonder Real Managers are frustrated about the lack of such clear solutions in their fuzzy, unclear real world. First, the activities of RMs are much more diverse. In addition, implementing all five of Fayol's functions often takes more clout than most RMs have.

Fayol subdivided his five functions into 14 more specific principles of management. These seemingly clear, universal principles may have worked for Fayol way back when, but are certainly not so precise or valid in today's practice:

1. *Division of Work.* Specialization makes functional division of the organization and functionally oriented education and training possible. In fact, work is never perfectly divided either by required effort or skills. When Real Managers control resources essential to do their work, they have more power than others who control fewer, or less important, resources. Hence, the division of work is affected by both functional (the need to get the job done) considerations, as described by Fayol, and political (power and control) considerations. Real Managers address the latter through their networking activities.

2. *Equal Authority and Responsibility.* If managers have responsibility for a given area, they should have the commensurate
authority to carry it out. In fact, Real Managers are usually
restricted on both counts. They often have limited control over
the consequences if subordinates do not perform. Most RMs
today do not directly control the hiring, firing, pay, or promotion of their subordinates. This again means Real Managers
must cope with the problem by maximizing their own reservoir
of human resource management and networking skills.

3. *Discipline.* Obedience and outward respect and civility are two
tenets of traditional management that still seem to be relevant,
if not always present, in many of the organizations we studied. Our trained observers did note that their target managers
did discipline employees, but for privacy issues they were not
allowed (by us or the Real Manager) to directly observe the content of the discipline being delivered. Thus, although it would
have been interesting, we did not include this activity in our
analysis.

4. *Unity of Command.* The one-boss principle is really a myth in
many of the organizations we studied. RMs in our study complained that they were frequently subject to orders from anyone
above them—not just their assigned boss. This caused much
confusion, stress, and depending on the style of the upper-level
manager giving the order, anger and resentment. They often
blamed their direct boss for letting this happen and not "cover-
ing my back."

5. *Unity of Direction.* Groups or individuals with the same purposes and objectives are ideal: clear, visionary, forceful organizational missions are crucial to effective management. But we
rarely found this kind of unity of direction in the organizations
and RMs we studied.

6. *Subordination of Personal Interest to General Interest.* In the
short run, this principle of traditional management may hold,
and certainly may prevail at the team level, but in the long run it
denies the realities of human behavior. We found that RMs who,
by all appearances, seemed ideally selfless were still operating
from a base of educated self-interest. In effect, they exchange

short-term for long-term returns. Long-run subordination of RMs' self- interest may be unrealistic in contemporary society: it would require them to be irrationally oblivious to their own interests.

7. *Remuneration of Personnel.* The value of the manager to the organization still determines how much they are paid, as adjusted for labor market conditions. However, as in the private sector as a whole, the RMs in our study sometimes complained about their pay and noted the outlandish compensation received by the heads of their organizations. The logic of market conditions doesn't apply equally to everyone.

8. *Centralization.* Directly related to the principle of Equal Authority and Responsibility, this principle states that when the mid-level RM's job becomes important enough, upper-level management eventually relinquishes sufficient power to the RM to get the job done—ideally. RMs in our study had to deal with the real world, however, and many told us they felt responsible for results but not empowered enough to get the job done, especially if results fell short of their boss's expectations.

9. *Scalar Chain.* The chain, a clear hierarchy of management, exists, but Real Managers supplement it by crossing department and division boundaries in day-to-day activities. Without networking relationships and dotted lines that connect managers outside the chain, probably nothing in these organizations would get done.

10. *Order.* With a degree of order in management, we should expect people and things to be in logical places. In Fayol's ideal, everything would be exactly in its proper place: RMs with their specific offices, all equipment residing in proper storage locations—a place for everything, and everything in its place. In our study, on the contrary, because of the dynamic nature of many of the organizations we studied, chaos, not order, reigns supreme.

11. *Equity.* Employees demand fairness (on balance, although not necessarily on every issue) as *they* see it. We found that RMs generally practiced this sort of fairness on a day-to-day basis, but when pressed could not give examples of taking positive affirmative action in pursuit of it, although they gave lip service

to their support of the assimilation of women and minorities into the mainstream of their organizations, and to their support of equal opportunity for all.

12. *Stability of Tenure of Personnel.* Real Managers should seek to develop cadres of subordinates committed to long-term employment. Japanese firms with their lifetime employment policies illustrate this principle, and there is evidence that many American firms are also committed to long-term personnel stability. However, rapidly changing technology, resistance to change (by the organization as well as by individual employees), and overhead costs of employee medical and retirement benefits seem to drive many Real Managers to pursue short-run or intermediate (rather than long-term) workforce objectives.

13. *Initiative.* RMs should be encouraged to be self-activating. Tom Peters, of *In Search of Excellence* fame, feels strongly that constant innovation is a basic requirement for successful, effective management. Our study showed that most RMs find themselves in dynamically changing situations today, but generally seem unaware of the inherent potential for initiative and innovation that exists in this kind of situation.

14. *Esprit De Corps.* Harmony and commitment among employees are the objectives of this final Fayolian principle. Some of the organizations we studied had flirted with organization development (OD) and quality of work/life (QWL) programs. RMs in our study mostly reacted positively to these programs, but felt they didn't last long enough to make an impact. Other things, such as budgets and cutbacks, too often took precedence.

Other classical management theorists and all the introductory management textbooks in the field today list similar principles to follow for managerial success and effectiveness. The language has changed over the years, but the principles have stayed the same. If you look beyond the close orbit of management theory, you'll find a wider galaxy of theories about good management. In fact, there are probably as many ideas about what managers should do, as there are managers—maybe more! Prescriptions and advice have been offered not only by management scholars and writers but also by psychologists, sociologists, economists, political scientists, business scholars in finance and marketing, and sometimes even practicing managers themselves. To the recognized founding father Fayol, and many management gurus since, these were clear principles that should have worked in the real world. To RMs, they are too often fictitious or even chimerical. Whatever their origin, they remain theories, and too often management theories don't really apply for the frontline manager down in the weeds.

The late management theorist Harold Koontz described the widely divergent principles and theories of management as a "jungle," and described six schools of management that outlined a map out of the jungle. We like to call Koontz's six schools of thought *waterholes* in the management jungle—conveniently placed points that structure the tangled journey towards managerial effectiveness. However, they don't always replicate the RM's actual day-to-day work environment. As usual, in practice things get messy.

Waterhole No. 1: The Management Process School. This approach begins by identifying functions of managers, in accord with Fayol's plan, organize, command, coordinate, and control. It then asks questions about the nature, purpose, structure, and processes of each function and formulates universal principles, similar to Fayol's fourteen principles. But like those principles, this approach often devolves into unrealistic platitudes for Real Managers.

Waterhole No. 2: The Empirical School. This is an experiential approach, based on cases and observations of what worked in the past, and what might work when reapplied in the future. Management scholars used this approach to regenerate supposedly universal principles of management, by following the same steps as the management process approach. If we duplicated this case approach, the return on investment for RMs would not be very great.

Waterhole No. 3: The Human Behavior School. This approach centers on interpersonal relations, in the guise of human relations, organizational behavior, leadership, or organizational psychology. We found this to be a good approach for some of the problems facing today's Real Managers, and it is becoming more important as technology has recently taken precedence and outstripped the management of human resources.

Waterhole No. 4: The Social System School. This approach focuses on social dynamics and networks, and organizational cultural issues. It goes beyond the sterile formal organization. Essentially, the approach seeks to apply the principles of basic sociology to management: the interactions between individuals and groups, and what those interactions mean. Unfortunately, with the exception of the recent emergence of the positive and negative impact of social media, Real Managers have not yet been able to translate much of such behavioral science knowledge into action. Therefore, it doesn't offer real protection from day-to-day threats facing RMs in the jungle.

Waterhole No. 5: The Decision Theory School. This school emphasizes quantifying (assigning numbers to) management problems or courses of action and rationally selecting the best, or optimal, solution. Drawing from economics, this approach springs from problems in utility maximization, indifference curves, marginal utility, and risk/uncertainty behavior. Such a strictly numerical approach offers protection to RMs from some, but certainly not all, threats in the management jungle.

Waterhole No. 6: The Mathematical School. This approach focuses on using mathematical and industrial engineering logic to express and solve problems in management. Unfortunately, RMs aren't able to reduce their problems to such logical models and optimal solutions. Perhaps too much of what happens in the day-to-day activities of Real Managers is illogical, if for no other reason than lack of information. Again, mathematics can help save RMs from some, but not all, of the perils of the management jungle.

Can we escape from the jungle of confusion? Taking the extreme of going all in on any one of the schools seems unwise. If we view each management approach as correct unto itself, then we will discard whatever may be useful in each of the rejected approaches. The other extreme view, that we must take a global view of *everything* offered by *all* of the approaches and that none of it will be of value unless and until we make it all work together, also seems fruitless. Each of these extremes heads us right back into the jungle.

The correct path is to use the benefits of each approach, but first to determine what successful and effective RMs *really* do before we endorse prescriptive approaches of what managers *should* do. In this way, theory is tempered by what Real Managers *actually* do. The standard analysis of managerial success has always assumed that certain personal traits and/or managerial activities *cause* managers to succeed. We have found instead that what successful RMs *actually* do also differs from what traditional management literature says they *should* do in order to be successful.

Over the years, there are probably as many ideas and prescriptions about what a manager should do to be successful as there are writings on the subject. These range all the way from a Dale Carnegie course brochure to a research-based article or book on organizational behavior. The definition of managerial success becomes crucial. Although it is easy to deride the fluff of simplistic "how-to" approaches to success, research-based, scholarly writings can be just as misleading and irrelevant to Real Managers (for example, the continuing debate in academic circles over rigor vs. relevance has no bearing for most people).

In some organizations under some conditions, task/technically-oriented managers prosper and are successful; in other organizations, and even in the same organization under different conditions, a manager using such a style cannot even survive. This finding holds for people-oriented managers as well. The so-called contingency approach to management tries to account for these situational differences, but does it mean, as one RM put it, that "the way managers succeed makes no sense"? Or could it mean that a given style or behavior or activity affects success only indirectly?

Willy Loman, the infamous lead character in the classic *Death of a Salesman*, defined success as whether or not the manager ". . . was well liked." We may question the merit of such a simplistic definition of managerial success, but when researchers ask subordinates in a questionnaire to report subjectively on their managers, they are really using the same approach suggested by Willy's definition of success.

Who decides whether a manager is successful? In the conventional textbook and research arena, academics typically depend on prior evidence and their own best judgment to decide what personal characteristics and managerial activities determine success. Similarly, practicing managers use their experience and best judgment to deduce those characteristics and activities. But in reality, practicing managers don't have the time, or don't take the time, to define what makes a manager successful because they are too busy putting out fires and, hopefully, getting the job done. Rightly or wrongly, they believe that events eventually will determine managerial success at the bottom line. The problem with both academic and practitioner approaches to managerial success is that they are based on assumptions, or, at best, quasi-empirical evidence from questionnaires, leavened by experience and even intuition. Let's re-examine some of these common assumptions about managerial success. As we will see throughout the rest of the book, they are belied by our findings about successful RMs.

CHAPTER **THREE**
The Study

WHAT DO REAL MANAGERS DO? THE ANSWERS TO THIS simple question are complex, and require the kind of layered study we designed. First, we deployed trained observers to freely observe and carefully record all the behaviors and activities of forty-four managers in their natural settings. These were Real Managers: they held bona fide managerial positions and all had people working directly for them. They came from all levels (lower, middle, and upper management) and all types of organizations (including manufacturing plants, retail stores, hospitals, corporate headquarters, a railroad, government agencies, insurance companies, a newspaper office, and financial institutions).

Most empirically based studies of leadership and management have depended almost solely upon data from standardized questionnaires and interviews. Direct observational studies of managerial activities in a natural setting, on the other hand, have been extremely rare. The one that received the most attention was strategy guru Henry Mintzberg's observational study of five chief executive officers (CEOs) over five-day periods, conducted in the early 1970s. Mintzberg categorized his CEOs into ten possible managerial roles:

1. *Figurehead*—doing ritual, ceremonial or symbolic tasks.
2. *Leader*—guiding, hiring, firing, training, praising, promoting, and evaluating.
3. *Liaison*—maintaining connections outside the work unit.
4. *Monitor*—keeping abreast of information.

5. *Disseminator*—passing information to subordinates.
6. *Spokesperson*—representing work unit interests to upper-level management.
7. *Entrepreneur*—initiating controlled change in the work unit.
8. *Disturbance Handler*—handling crises.
9. *Resources Allocator*—controlling money, employees, material, equipment, facilities, and services.
10. *Negotiator*—committing organizational resources to and from the work unit; this can apply to unions, contracts, other organizations.

Mintzberg also identified five distinguishing characteristics of the managers he studied:

1. They work at a relentless pace, seldom taking a break. Upper-level managers often take their work home, and most are obsessive about their jobs.
2. They spend brief amounts of time on fragmented activities, and are frequently interrupted. These characteristics are more pronounced at lower management levels.
3. They tend to direct their attention to concrete issues and to the most current information, rather than attending to reflective planning.
4. They spend one-third of their time communicating with people outside the company and a third to a half of their time communicating with subordinates.
5. They conduct two-thirds of their communications orally, mostly by telephone or at unscheduled meetings.

Mintzberg's study was pioneering because he used observational methods but, more importantly, his findings contradicted traditional beliefs, as well as the body of literature about what managers do or should do. But it wasn't enough, particularly because it focused on only five CEOs instead of a much broader swathe of managers—Real Managers, in other words.

Besides the Mintzberg study, there have been only a few other observational studies of managerial work. Harvard Professor John Kotter's study of 15 general managers conducted in the early 1980s was the most prominent. Supplementing many hours of observation with questionnaires and interviews, Kotter found that his managers' work environments were organized by a series of specific job demands, which included:

1. Setting basic goals and policies in an uncertain environment.
2. Balancing the allocation of scarce resources among a wide range of users while protecting long-term goals.
3. Monitoring and controlling complex activities in order to recognize and fix problems quickly.
4. Getting information, cooperation, and support from upper-level management to do the job, and demanding support without alienating upper-level managers.
5. Getting cooperation from corporate staff, unions, and big customers to overcome resistance, red tape, and other obstacles.
6. Motivating subordinates and controlling unacceptable performance and interdepartmental conflicts.

Many of Kotter's job demands resemble Mintzberg's roles. Overall, however, Kotter stressed that his general managers have two common activities—agenda-setting and networking. This intriguing finding paints a clearer picture of the day-to-day requirements placed on managers. Kotter's agenda-setting was a type of "reflective planning" that Mintzberg said managers don't do, and even though networking is similar to informal politicking, Mintzberg did not address it directly.

As important as they were, however, Mintzberg and Kotter's studies were limited to a very small number of only high-level managers in restricted settings. We needed a much more comprehensive study that delved deep into the day-to-day work lives of mid-level managers—Real Managers. To get there, we gathered data on literally hundreds of managers from numerous diverse organizations. Also unlike the multitude of previous studies in the fields of organizational behavior and human resource management, we did not depend on a single method to gather the data. Over a four-year period, we used both free observation and systematic participant observation in natural work settings, supplemented by intensive interviews and standardized questionnaires. We carefully analyzed the data throughout the study to monitor its reliability and validity.[1]

We observed Real Managers in the initial phase of the study in a completely unstructured format, for a varied hour each day over a two-week period (i.e., 440 hours of unstructured, on-the-job observation of RMs). The 44 observers in this first phase of the study participated in an extensive training workshop; we wanted to make sure our observers avoided the systemic errors common to this kind of monitoring. By writing observation logs from several role-playing exercises that we critiqued, the trainees learned how to observe the behavior of the target RM continuously over an hour and to record all specific, identifiable behaviors and activities in their logs. They were taught to be reporters, concentrating on objective description rather than prejudging or evaluating the behaviors and activities they observed.

The observers systematically varied their hours throughout each working day during the two weeks to make sure they represented all parts of the workday. After two weeks, we shared copies of the logs on their behaviors and activities with our 44 RMs and asked them to rate to what extent these were typical of their day-to-day behavior and activities. On a scale of 1 to 5, the average was about 4, indicating that these descriptions were typical "to a considerable extent." In other words, the RMs told us that these logs were accurate depictions of their day-to-day work lives.

This first unstructured observation phase was only a prelude, however, to establishing specific categories of management activities, by which we structured the observation system that observers used to gather data for the heart of the study. We had to carefully craft these categories to accurately reflect the range of RM work activities.

We based our categories on the Delphi method, which the RAND Corporation first developed and used during the heyday of its think tank phase in the 1950s. The Delphi method consists of using members of a panel to make independent, autonomous judgments. These judgments are then summarized and fed back to the panel members. The panel members, using the composite feedback, then make further anonymous

---

1 For the interested reader, the supplemental readings and references listed at the back of the book cite various journal articles that describe in detail the various aspects (sample sizes, reliabilities, validity analysis, etc.) of the study.

judgments. Our Delphi panel had seven members, four from the research team and three relatively uninformed members. We selected them specifically because they had no prior knowledge of the management literature or practical management experience, and thus were unbiased. From this unbiased starting point, we trained the panel members, starting with the Delphi method itself and continuing with training in how to construct adequate behavioral categories from raw data.

In the first Delphi round, the panel members independently reviewed the extensive logs completed by the 44 observers, and put together about 100 general categories of managerial activity with accompanying behavioral descriptors. These categories were independently fed back to each of the panelists with accompanying anonymous comments. Through several iterations, the panelists continued to reduce the categories into smaller but more comprehensive sets. Table 3-1 shows the final 12 categories and the accompanying behavioral descriptors.

The categories in Table 3-1 represent the free observation data on the 44 RMs initially studied. They are comprehensive, use generally recognized terminology, and are mutually exclusive.

TABLE 3-1

The Categories and Behavioral Descriptors Derived from Free Observations of Forty-four RMs.[2]

PLANNING	STAFFING
• setting goals and objectives • defining tasks needed to accomplish goals • scheduling employees, timetables • assigning tasks and providing routine instructions • coordinating activities of different subordinates to keep work running smoothly • organizing the work	• developing job descriptions for position openings • reviewing applications • interviewing applicants • hiring • contacting applicants to inform them of hiring decision • "filling in" where needed

TRAINING/DEVELOPING	DECISION MAKING
• orienting employees, arranging for training seminars, etc. • clarifying roles, duties, job descriptions • coaching, mentoring, walking subordinates through task • helping subordinate with personal development plans	• defining problems • choosing between two or more alternatives or strategies • handling day-to-day operational crises as they arise • weighing the tradeoffs; cost/benefit analysis • making the decision • developing new procedures to increase efficiency

HANDLING PAPERWORK	EXCHANGING INFORMATION
• processing mail • reading reports, in-box • writing reports, memos, letters, etc. • doing routing financial reporting and bookkeeping • doing general desk work	• answering routine procedural questions • receiving and disseminating requested information • conveying results of meetings • giving or receiving routine information over the phone • holding staff meetings of an informational nature (e.g., status updates, new company policies, etc.)

CONTROLLING	MOTIVATING/REINFORCING
• inspecting work • walking around • monitoring performance data (e.g., computer printouts, production, financial reports) • practicing preventive maintenance	• allocating formal organizational rewards • asking for input, participation • conveying appreciation, compliments • giving credit where due • listening to suggestions • giving positive performance feedback • increasing job challenge • delegating responsibility and authority • letting subordinates determine how to do their own work • supporting the group before superiors and others, backing a subordinate

2 Adapted from Fred Luthans and Diane Lockwood, "Toward an Observation System for Measuring Leader Behavior in Natural Settings," in J.G. Hunt, D. Hosking, C. Schriesheim, and R. Stewart, eds., *Leaders and Managers* (New York: Pergamon, 1984), p. 122. This article makes a detailed statistical assessment of the reliability and validity of these categories of leader behavior.

DISCIPLINING/PUNISHING	INTERACTING WITH OUTSIDERS
• enforcing rules and policies • glaring, nonverbal harassing • demoting, firing, laying off employee • issuing any formal organizational reprimand or notice • "chewing out" a subordinate, criticizing • giving negative performance feedback	• public relations • contacts with customers • contacts with suppliers, vendors • external meetings • community service activities

MANAGING CONFLICT	SOCIALIZING/POLITICKING
• managing interpersonal conflict between subordinates or others • appealing to higher authority to resolve a dispute • appealing to third-party negotiators • seeking cooperation or consensus between conflicting parties • attempting to resolve conflicts between subordinate and self	• engaging in nonwork-related chitchat (e.g. family or personal matters) • "joking around" • discussing rumors, hearsay, grapevine • complaining, griping, downgrading others • politicking, gamesmanship

Finally, we organized the 12 categories into the four comprehensive activities shown in Figure 3-1. This, then, is what Real Managers do: they (1) communicate, (2) manage through traditional means, (3) network, and (4) engage in human resource management. For years, the management literature has played armchair quarterback, creating normative management functions straight from theory, out of whole cloth. We did something very different in our study. Starting from what our team observed, we derived—empirically—the real activities of Real Managers.

FIGURE 3-1
Real Managers' Activities
(n=44 RMs using free-observation data)

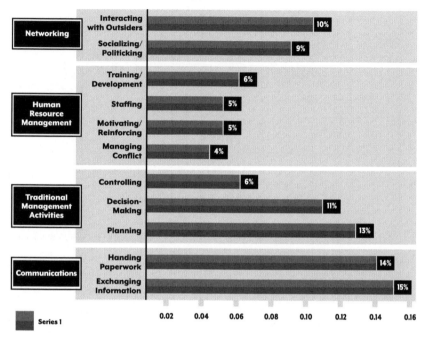

The managerial activities identified in Table 3-1 and Figure 3-1 provided a foundation and point of departure for our study of Real Managers. However, to provide follow-up and to get more intensive descriptions of and rich qualitative data on these activities, we next conducted 165 interviews with a completely different set of Real Managers. Like the first set of 44, these 165 RMs came from all levels and all types of organizations. The trained interviewers first asked subordinates for examples of their immediate boss's behavior in each of the 12 categories of managerial work.

The interviewers asked for a specific incident that represented a great, an average, and a low amount of the given activity. Using a systematic retranslation method to sort these incidents, a team of researchers and practicing RMs reduced the incidents to the ones most representative of each category. Table 3-2 summarizes these representative, real incidents. In combination, the free observation of the 44 RMs and interviews with subordinates about the 165 RMs provide a comprehensive, accurate, and finely-tuned picture of what managers really do.

TABLE 3-2
Specific Behavioral Incidents of Real Managers' Activities

TYPE OF ACTIVITY	DESCRIPTIVE CATEGORY	AMOUNT	BEHAVIORAL INCIDENT DERIVED FROM INTERVIEWS
Networking	Interacting with Outsiders	High	· Seeks involvement in public relations activities, such as attending community events. · Handles customer/client relations with other organizations in the industry and meets with members of clubs important to the organization.
		Medium	· Gives presentations at service clubs or similar organizations. · Has lunch with suppliers of materials to discuss how things are going.
		Low	· Takes phone calls or goes through emails from suppliers. · Talks with customers or clients who ask about a product or service.
	Socializing/ Politicking	High	· Entertains top-level managers in the organization, with activities such as playing tennis or going fishing with them. · Keeps an active social calendar and possibly holds an open house with food and drink for employees.
		Medium	· Socializes with the employees before a staff meeting begins. · Socializes with employees in the company lounge or other gathering places.
		Low	· Talks with peers and subordinates in the cafeteria during lunch. · Has a cup of coffee with the staff.
Human Resource Management	Motivating/ Reinforcing	High	· Immediately compliments a subordinate who handles an irate customer or client very well. · Sends a email praising an employee who has done an excellent job.
		Medium	· Compliments an employee before co-workers at a staff meeting or in the presence of other managers. · Has individual discussions with subordinates to compliment them on work they have done well.
		Low	· Says to an employee, "Now that is really good," after hearing about a customer encounter. · Tells an employee, in passing, that he or she had a good week or did a good job on some task.
	Disciplining/ Punishing	High	· Suspends an employee without pay for unsatisfactory performance. · Writes a reprimand, sends copies to the employee and the personnel department, and uses this information in determining the employee's annual wage increase.

(continued on next page)

TYPE OF ACTIVITY	DESCRIPTIVE CATEGORY	AMOUNT	BEHAVIORAL INCIDENT DERIVED FROM INTERVIEWS
		Medium	• Places an employee on probation for recurrent lateness. • Writes a formal notice of undesirable actions by an employee, gives a copy to the employee, and puts one in their personnel file.
		Low	• Reprimands an employee for occasional lateness or for a performance problem. • Raises her or his voice at an employee for surfing the internet on company time.
	Managing Conflict	High	• Explains the reasons for decision to co-workers upset because one worker received a promotion. • Talks face-to-face with two employees whose functions overlap when one of them believes the other receives too much recognition or salary, listens to both, and sorts out the facts.
		Medium	• Personally talks to subordinates who are not getting along • Mediates when two subordinates are having a disagreement about the date when a new procedure should start.
		Low	• Separates employees to avoid further argument • Responds to employee complaints about a personality problem with another employee.
	Staffing	High	• When filling a position, considers in-house personnel for promotion, reviews outside applications, holds interviews, reviews information, and makes the selection decision. • Designs job descriptions, screens applications, interviews applicants, and selects the new employee.
		Medium	• Sets wages and benefits for a new employee, after the hiring decision is made. • Checks past work experience of applicants who appear to be acceptable.
		Low	• Makes the decision to hire a new employee or interviews the new employee on the first day of work. • Goes outside of company to find replacements who meet certain criteria.
	Training/ Developing	High	• Brings in experts as part of arranging professional-development programs for employees. • Coaches the staff on necessary work processes, organizes presentations of procedures, and involves the staff in practical training exercises.
		Medium	• Conducts in-house meetings to review specific techniques or procedures. • Teaches the more difficult jobs, such as operating complex equipment or tasks which require coordination with other workers, to certain employees.
		Low	• Gives subordinates job descriptions and written procedures from which to learn their responsibilities. • Performs a periodic update of a training manual.

TYPE OF ACTIVITY	DESCRIPTIVE CATEGORY	AMOUNT	BEHAVIORAL INCIDENT DERIVED FROM INTERVIEWS
Communication	Exchanging Routine Information	High	· Every week has a scheduled meeting with subordinates, shares ideas, and leads a discussion about new methods and procedures. · After meeting with other managers, distributes the meeting's notes to subordinates.
		Medium	· Learns of a change, walks into the general office or work area, and announces it. · Holds a monthly meeting to pass on data received at staff meetings attended with other managers.
		Low	· Posts notices on bulletin board for employees to read. · Circulates an interoffice memo with no requests for response or feedback.
	Handling Paperwork	High	· Prepares daily, weekly, and monthly reports, which include cost reports and comparisons with past records and activities. · Pays bills, submits orders, completes payroll checks, and compares cash receipts or similar data.
		Medium	· Records figures from work units several times a day and records the totals at the end of the day. · Reads the daily mail and routes it to employees.
		Low	· Checks correspondence, such as incoming mail and advertising. · Signs attendance reports.
Traditional Management	Planning	High	· Sets goals and then holds face-to-face meetings with workers, giving specific instructions, review dates, and deadlines. · Reviews past budgets, operations data, and expense figures, consults with other departments, and then sets specific goals for the next year.
		Medium	· Develops a work schedule for a given project. · Assigns employees for different jobs and time schedules.
		Low	· Budgets time between departments or work areas. · Assigns employees the materials, tools, and equipment they need to do the job.
	Decision-making	High	· Reads all facts related to the problem or issue and discusses the facts with others involved. Considers short- and long-term impacts, makes recommendations to higher management, and implements final decisions. · Makes a judgment on a major acquisition, an important policy change, or a new service or product.
		Medium	· Notices a problem, discusses it with another supervisor or with specialists in the area, and then selects a course of action. · Delegates the problem to someone closer to the situation and then receives a follow-up report or phone call on the situation.

(continued on next page)

TYPE OF ACTIVITY	DESCRIPTIVE CATEGORY	AMOUNT	BEHAVIORAL INCIDENT DERIVED FROM INTERVIEWS
		Low	• Delegates or refers minor problems or situations to the next person in line. • Reviews the situation and tells a subordinate, "You'll have to handle it."
	Controlling	High	• Makes personal visits to work areas in different departments or units on a scheduled basis to check work progress and compares summaries or employees' performance to standards. • Reviews the time already spent and the time remaining on projects and meets with employees to control efficiency problems.
		Medium	• Checks to see how long it took to do a job and to inspect finished products or services. • Reviews reports and performance of routine functions to ensure they are running smoothly and goes over reports with employees.
		Low	• Phones or emails to check on operations. • Tours the office to see if people are working and to check on equipment.

Once we were satisfied that the free, unstructured observation of 44 RMs in their natural settings, the interviews with 165 other RMs, and the representative incidents provided an accurate answer to what Real Managers do, we turned our attention to the relative occurrence of the activities. We used a completely different set of data to analyze the relative frequencies of the RMs' activities. Specifically, we aggregated three waves (three points in time, each about a year apart) of structured observational data on 248 RMs from all levels and types of organizations. To gather these data, trained participant observers filled out a managerial activities checklist, based on Table 3-1, 80 times over a two-week period. These observations took place during a predetermined but random 10-minute period of each working hour over the two weeks. The participant observers for this third data set were selected on the basis of their being able to see and hear the target RM at all times, as well as having a deep understanding of the functions, terminology, and nature of the work performed by the target RM.

We should pause here to describe the extensive training workshop that we conducted for the participant observers in this phase, because the results we obtained were so striking. We intended the workshop to train observers how to gather their data as carefully, accurately, and unobtrusively as possible. We told them that the data would not only assist the research, but would also be used for executive development purposes, and that their findings would always be kept anonymous. We went through the observation form in detail, paying special attention to defining and interpreting the behavioral categories, and ways to overcome potential observation errors. Finally, we trained the observers to be as unobtrusive as possible when recording RM behavior, and to keep the targeted RMs unaware of both the timing of the observations and the nature of the behavioral categories. Because we used *participant* observers who were in constant contact with the targeted RMs, we wanted to minimize intrusiveness in recording their behaviors.

The second half of the training was devoted to modeling and actual practice through role playing. To evaluate the training, we presented an elaborate skit that included six predetermined managerial activities to the trainees (they identified these activities correctly over 90% of the time, with an overall mean accuracy of 92.5%). As we indicated when discussing discipline, because for privacy reasons our trained participant observers were unable to observe the disciplining/punishing activity directly, we deleted this activity from later study and from our analysis of the relative frequencies of the managerial activities. We know from our interview data that this activity is done, but (mercifully) our observers were generally unable to record it. The inference to be drawn here is that most disciplining/punishing is done rarely and in private.

Figure 3-2 depicts how RMs divide their time and effort among the 11 descriptive managerial activities from Table 3-1, displaying average frequencies for the observed 248 RMs at all levels. However, upon further analysis we discovered that some activities are sensitive to the level of the RM. For example, bottom-level Real Managers have the least opportunity to do the traditional management activity of planning, or the networking activity of interacting with outsiders. We'll examine some of these differences between top-, middle-, and first-level managers in more detail in Chapter Four.

FIGURE 3-2
Distribution of Real Managers' Activities

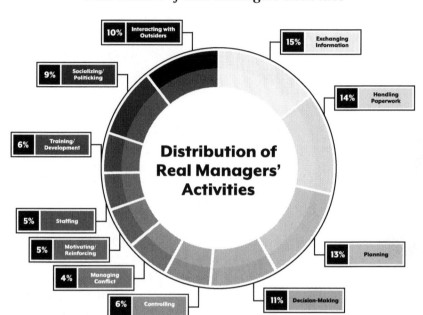

As shown in Figure 3-2, Real Managers spend almost a third of their time and effort in communication activities (exchanging information and handling paperwork). Another third is spent in traditional management activities (planning, decision-making, and controlling). That leaves about a fifth of their time and effort for networking activities (interacting with outsiders and socializing/politicking), and a fifth for human resource management activities (motivating/reinforcing, staffing, training/developing, and managing conflict). Figure 3-3 shows the relative distribution of these four aggregated activities. This is a more definitive answer to the question, "What do Real Managers do?"

FIGURE 3-3
Distribution of Real Managers' Activities, Summarized

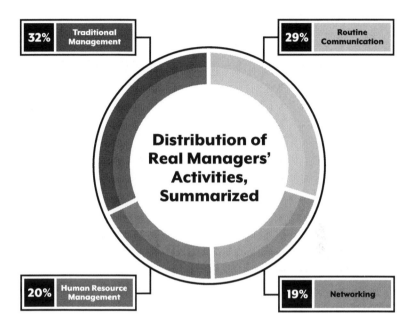

It turns out that RMs spend a lot of their time in routine communication and traditional management activities, which agrees with the conventional wisdom about managers. But this conclusion still conflicts somewhat with both Mintzberg's and Kotter's findings. For example, Mintzberg concluded that his CEOs did not do planning, as he defined it, and Kotter concluded that his general managers really did little decision-making. Contrary to common notions, however, we found that Real Managers devote a relatively significant amount of their time to dealing with human resource management and engaging in networking—two activities which have been virtually ignored in the traditional management literature.[3]

---

3 Kotter's study is an exception: he does include networking activities in his discussion of general managers. The behaviorally oriented literature, of course, focuses on human resource management activities.

THE STUDY OF SUCCESS

What do successful managers do? In traditional management literature, as well as to the person on the street, the meaning of "success" for managers varies widely. It's crucial, then, to answer the question with empirical research. Unlike our preliminary work with hundreds of RMs from many different types of organizations, the success portion of the study required more control, so we drew from a sample of 52 RMs from a limited number of organizations. We used this sample to determine if the type of organization or the level of the manager made a difference in relative success. In addition, we analyzed an additional sample of 79 RMs drawn from a broader range of organizations and found similar results to the more focused sample of 52.[4] That is, both the focused sample and a broader sample showed that managers' success was impacted in the same ways by typical managerial activities.

Before starting the study of successful RMs, we reasoned that a consensus about what success is would always be what the scholar or the practitioner thinks that success should be. In other words, success is in the eye of the beholder. We further reasoned that each organization has its own measure of managerial success, that the most successful managers are those most valued by their organizations, and that each organization rewards its most successful managers according to its own definition of success. Organizations do this, substantively and directly, by promoting their employees. Therefore, we measured managerial success by using an indicator of what the employing organization has already declared to be "success": how fast they promoted managers.

We derived this Manager Success Index (MSI) from previous approaches scholars have used to determine either promotion velocity or manager achievement. In our study, we objectively calculated the MSI for each RM in our sample based on the level of the RM in the organization divided by the RM's tenure in the organization.[5] One of the first arguments against such a measure as the MSI is that it does not account for new hires at high levels, who clearly have a short tenure

---

4 It should be emphasized that these samples were drawn from the 248 RMs whose behavior was recorded by the trained participant observers. Thus, the observers were blind to whether the target RMs were defined as successful or not.

5 The interested reader may want to refer to the Luthans, Rosenkrantz, and Hennessey (1986) article cited in the supplemental readings and references for a more detailed description of the MSI.

with the organization. However, remember that most organizations assess the value of new hires before employing them; in other words, they interview them (much more on this process later in the book). By the organization's own definition, the new hire, under such conditions, has greater perceived value and thus, potentially, the rewards that come with that value (that is, success), than longer tenured in-house managers. Otherwise, the organization would have promoted the longer tenured managers faster. Therefore, high MSIs for newly hired managers are not unlikely. The MSI is also useful because middle- or even lower level managers also could be "successful" as measured by this index, depending on how long they had been with the organization.

After all this definitional and preparatory work, our analysis of successful Real Managers proceeded in several directions. In the first part of our investigation we identified the specific managerial activities that statistically were related to success (using multiple regression techniques) as defined by the MSI. We also looked at whether the type of organization or the level of the RM made a difference in success. Next, we did a descriptive comparison of the activities of the most successful third of the RMs in the organizations we studied with the activities of the least successful third. Because we wanted to analyze only RMs who were clearly successful or unsuccessful, we left the middle third out of the comparison analysis. We also compared what activities top-level RMs are engaged in with those that mid-level and first-level RMs do. Finally, we determined the relative strength of each of the managerial activities, related to RMs' success.

We have cross-checked the effects on our findings using MSI, relative pay, and level, but disregarding tenure in the organization, and have found comparable results to the MSI analysis that included tenure. However, successful managers, as defined by the MSI, may be at the top, middle or lower levels of their organizations. In other words, the study deems an RM who is at the third level from the top but has been with the company for only six years to be more successful than another RM at the second level who has been with the company for 20 years. It's the speed of promotion that counts most. (In addition, in some of our analyses of successful managers, we simply defined the CEO, the head of the organization, as being successful.) Here's an example, by the numbers, to illustrate. To reiterate, we calculated the success index by dividing the RMs' level in their respective organization (e.g., 1 for the CEO, 4 or 5 for a first-line supervisor depending on how many levels in the given organization) by their tenure in the organization. So, using this measure of success, an RM at the fourth level of the organization who had been there a total of eight years would be rated more successful than an RM at the third level who had been there for 15 years. In other words, this empirical measure of success is an index of the speed or velocity of promotion.

THE STUDY OF EFFECTIVENESS

What do *effective* managers do? For *success*, as we just described, we used an empirical definition (the MSI) drawn from observational data on a sample of 52 RMs from a limited number of organizations, but the process used to analyze effectiveness was somewhat different. Although we did do an effectiveness analysis of these same 52 RMs in order to make a direct comparison of successful versus effective RMs, this effectiveness part of the study also drew from a larger observational and questionnaire database collected over the four-year period.

The larger database was necessary for us in part because of the definition of effectiveness itself—or the multiplicity thereof. Simply put, "effective" is a hard thing to define, and both management theorists and managers themselves have spent decades coming up with different definitions and measures (for more on this definitional problem, see Chapter Five). Because of the definition controversy and the consequent (and inevitable) measurement problems it entailed, our effectiveness index was much more difficult to determine than the success index. In the end, however, we overcame many of the problems by using a combined or multiple measure of effectiveness, which we believed would be more valid than a single dimension.

Specifically, we used a combined, multiple measure containing three dimensions: (1) organizational unit effectiveness in terms of quantity and quality of performance, (2) subordinate satisfaction, and (3) subordinate organizational commitment. We used standardized questionnaires filled out by subordinates (the Mott Organizational Effectiveness Questionnaire, the Job Diagnostic Index, and the Organizational Commitment Questionnaire; see *Supplemental Readings and*

References for complete citations), all with high reliabilities generally, and in this study in particular, to measure the three dimensions of RM effectiveness. Thus, our data for effectiveness came from that collected by the participant observers on 178 RMs, as well as questionnaire data from their direct subordinates. This sample came from a large number of organizations, from all types of industries (manufacturing, retail, service, transportation, financial, and public organizations). We would have liked to use more quantitative measures like profits, or the quantity and quality of output or service. However, because we used a large sample of RMs in widely diverse jobs and organizations, we had to depend on standardized questionnaires.

Now, back to the original question: what do effective managers do? To determine this, we first calculated the average, or mean, of the squared correlations between the observed activities of the RMs and the combined effectiveness measure (organizational unit effectiveness and subordinate satisfaction and commitment) as determined by their direct subordinates. We then ordered these correlation-squared means in terms of their relative strengths. This gave us the relative contribution of each of the four activities to RMs' effectiveness and gave what we believed to be the best, most valid answer possible to the question of what effective RMs do. To summarize for the management scholars reading, our effectiveness analysis took the following steps: We squared the correlations between RM observed behavioral categories (those listed in Table 2-1) and the effectiveness measure (unit effectiveness, subordinate satisfaction, and subordinate commitment). We did this to approximate the amount of variance explained. These squared measures were averaged across samples.

We then established ratios between each observed RM behavior and the strongest related behavior (i.e. the highest squared number) in the set (for example, the strongest was 1.00, one half as strong would receive 0.5). We averaged these ratios across RM component behaviors that formed each of the four major activities (networking, traditional management, communicating, and human resource management). For example, the traditional management activities are represented by the averaged ratios for controlling, planning, and decision-making behaviors. We averaged rather than added the ratios to preclude our influencing the contributions of the activities. (If the ratios had been added, the activity with the highest number of component behaviors would have been the highest contributor to RM effectiveness.)

The sum of the activities was represented as 100% of that contributing to effectiveness. The resulting pie charts (Figures 3-1 and 3-2) indicate the relative strength of each activity contributing to RM effectiveness.

One could, of course, argue with our measures of effectiveness, or our use of correlational data (which, importantly, do *not* allow us to infer that these activities *cause* effectiveness) and relatively simple descriptive statistics. However, we would counter that the multiple methods (both observations and questionnaires) and multiple sources (both RMs and their subordinates) we used, not to mention multiple measures (organizational unit effectiveness, satisfaction, and commitment), gave us broad, detailed, and ultimately valid data on effectiveness. In addition, we would defend our use of relatively simple correlational and descriptive statistics instead of more sophisticated inferential statistics, because it is our intent to *describe* what effective RMs do. We did another analysis using questionnaire scales (for example, scales from the Leader Behavior Description Questionnaire, Managerial Behavior Survey, and Job Diagnostic Survey), which was, conceptually, related to the observed managerial activities, and found similar results. In other words, we had convergence between methods, in a large four-year study, to give confidence to our findings of what effective RMs do.

CHAPTER **FOUR**
Successful Real Managers

Jim is constantly seeking and nurturing contacts inside and outside the firm. He is always friendly and seems interested in your personal life. I like him and would do anything for him.

We get along real well in this department because we know George has such clout upstairs, as well as in the community, that no one is going to bother us.

JUST AS THERE HAS BEEN CONSIDERABLE LITERATURE ON what managers supposedly do, there has also been a great deal written over the years about the essential ingredients for managerial success. Our study raises serious questions about much of this literature. In this chapter, we delve into what actually makes a manager like Jim, described above, successful. As it turns out, Jim's *success* doesn't necessarily correspond to whether or not he is effective. However, nearly every management book presumes that effective performance is the goal, and that a manager's success goes hand-in-hand with being effective. Often the terms "successful" and "effective" are used interchangeably. We do not agree. With some exceptions, we have found major differences between what effective Real Managers do and what successful Real Managers do. In our study, "successful" and "effective" are not the same thing.

Being the best or most successful is the holy grail of management: as Lee Iacocca used to say, "What else is there?" But what constitutes "the best"? We have found common threads—common activities that RMs do to reach this high perch. The question then becomes "the best" for whom: the manager or the organization that employs the manager? Is the RMs' goal to be the most successful in their own career, or the most effective managers for organizational achievement? There have been surprisingly few attempts to carefully analyze managerial success. By concentrating on what Real Managers actually do, our study answered this question and exploded some of the prevailing myths surrounding how managers get ahead and get promoted.

Previous systematic observations of upper-level managers (like the Mintzberg and Kotter studies we described in the last chapter) haven't really focused on what Real Managers do, or been attuned to what constitutes success for the RM. Even the many biographies and autobiographies of prominent managers and leaders (people like elected government officials and cabinet members, as well as CEOs in the private sector such as Lee Iacocca of Chrysler, Henry Ford II, or ITT's Harold Geneen) don't isolate the elements of success. In addition, the little research that has been done on the nature of managerial work has often depended on survey questionnaires. When scholars like Mintzberg and Kotter have done direct observation, the sample sizes have been very small. Such studies don't allow comparison of the relative success of the managers studied. As we detailed in the last chapter, our study was different: besides its comprehensive coverage, it asked its subjects to talk about what they actually did. Our findings uncovered what RMs did every day that led to success. Just as important, we demystified the perception of success within RMs' organizations; in other words, how and why their peers saw our RMs as successful.

One of the most revealing and definitive findings of the entire study was the importance of networking to managerial success. Recall that we defined networking quite specifically as *interacting with outsiders* and *socializing and politicking*. We then broke each of these categories down into even more specific subcategories of behaviors. Interacting with outsiders, therefore, included interacting with customers, suppliers, and outside contacts; attending external meetings; and doing public relations and community service activities. For example, one successful RM told us he had a deliberate two-pronged strategy of calling on his supplier rather than always having the supplier call on him, and spending at least one afternoon a week visiting his customers, unannounced, to see what problems they were having with his firm's service. This same manager was on the board of the local YMCA and regularly attended the Rotary Club. He was engaged in all three behavioral subcategories of interacting with outsiders.

In the study, we defined *socializing and politicking* behaviorally as non-work-related "chit chat" concerning family or personal matters; informal joking; discussing rumors, hearsay, and the grapevine; complaining, griping, and downgrading others; and politicking and gamesmanship. Even apart from the formal analysis, our interviews and informal interactions with successful RMs and their subordinates showed us very clearly how skillful they were at socializing, politicking, and interacting with outsiders, and how much time they spent in this activity. One Real Manager elaborated:

> *People in this place get tired of always talking about business. They would rather talk about football or the latest rumor. I find that if I deliberately talk about these things either with my subordinates or the guy in the finance department, I can get in better with them and then call on them when I need them to meet a deadline or vote my way in a committee meeting.*

This successful RM participates in socializing and politicking in order to develop contacts, relationships, and reciprocal networks that magnify his available resources and ability to deliver when needed.

Statistical analysis clearly revealed that networking, more than any other management activity, was most closely related to managerial success. The "interacting with outsiders" dimension of networking was related to success in all the organizations we studied in the success analysis. "Socializing and politicking," on the other hand, was related to success more closely in entrepreneurial and results-oriented organizations than in bureaucratic and highly formalized organizations. This is not surprising. For example, when an organization needs to make an important decision and that decision is complicated and clouded by uncertainty (as is typical in an unstructured situation with little to no experience with formal policies or rules), managers try to influence the outcome through political maneuvering. When the decision is certain (as in a highly structured situation with considerable experience and formal policies or rules to cover it), those same managers make markedly fewer attempts to influence the outcome through socializing and politicking.

Our findings suggest that successful RMs do not dissipate their time and energies dealing with what they know to be uncontrollable variables.

Therefore, they would be expected to adapt their networking strategies to fit different types of organizations. Top-level managers tend to support this conclusion with how frequently—or infrequently—they exhibit these activities. For example, top-level RMs like CEOs interact with outsiders about as often as middle-level RMs, but nearly three times as often as first-level RMs. But the frequency is reversed for socializing and politicking. Middle-level and first-level RMs socialize and politick nearly three times as often as do the top-level RMs in our study. Socializing and politicking may have been necessary to get to the top, but once there, it seems, the RM can ease up on the constant gladhanding.

What else separated the most successful RMs from their counterparts they left behind? To find out, we did a simple descriptive/comparative analysis of management activities between the most successful (the top third on the velocity of promotion index) and the least successful (the bottom third on this index). It should be noted at the outset of this analysis that *all* of the RMs at all levels engaged in considerable amounts of all of the managerial activities that we measured. That is, they all did the traditional management activities of planning, decision-making, and controlling; communication activities of processing paperwork and exchanging routine information; networking activities of interacting with outsiders and socializing/politicking; and human resource management activities of managing conflict, staffing, training/developing, motivating/reinforcing, and disciplining/punishing. The difference lay in the amounts of these activities for more versus less successful RMs; we do not mean to imply that successful managers engaged in activities that less successful managers did not do at all (or vice versa).

With that caveat out of the way, we found significant differences in the amounts and frequencies of the managerial activities performed by the most successful RMs as opposed to their least successful counterparts. The bars in Figure 4-1 represent the percent of difference in frequencies of the managerial activities of the most successful compared to least successful RMs. Thus, Figure 4-1 indicates that the most successful RMs engage in routine communications 10% more than the least successful, and networking a huge 70% more. Conversely, the most successful RMs are doing 25% less human resources activities and 40% less traditional management activities than the least successful RMs.

FIGURE 4-1
Frequency of Managerial Activities,
More vs. Less Successful RMs

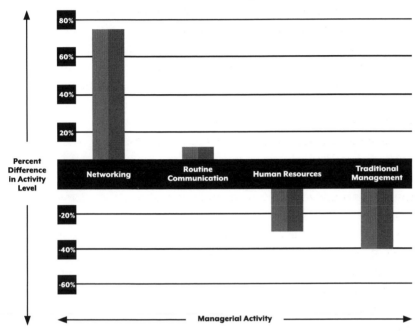

This analysis does not necessarily mean that the activities we mea-sured by directly observing the RMs guarantee more or less managerial success, or even that they are *sine qua non* prerequisites. Our findings could also mean that the directly observable activities we identified merely represent other, related characteristics that were not part of our study. For example, RMs who devote their energies to developing a power base through networking may be doing so because of their raw intelligence or perseverance (characteristics that many experts relate to managerial success). But, as we have said before, our study differs from previous research in that we used the frequency counts of directly observable activities of Real Managers in their day-to-day activities. In other words, we have the data, and it strongly indicates that all of these regular activities—things that you, the RM, do every day—are related to success and effectiveness in profound ways.

With the same sample of 52 managers that we used for the statistical and comparative analysis, we next determined the relative strengths of the various managerial activities' relationships to managerial success.[6] The results are in Figure 4-2, which shows these relative relationships. All of these activities contribute to RM success, but, taking a closer look, we see important differences among them.

What are those differences? To put it simply, some activities seem to contribute more to success than others. Networking activities once again had the strongest relationship to the success of RMs. Networking was followed, in turn, by communication, traditional management, and human resource management activities. A more detailed breakdown revealed that socializing/politicking had by far the strongest relationship, and interacting with outsiders was third. The communication activity of exchanging routine information was second.[7]

FIGURE 4-2
Relative Contributions of Managerial Activities to Success

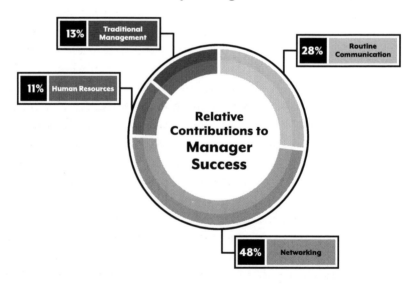

13% Traditional Management

28% Routine Communication

11% Human Resources

Relative Contributions to **Manager Success**

48% Networking

---

6 The technical details: we calculated the correlations squared between each of the 11 observed activities and the success index (MSI) and then rank-ordered these relationships in terms of their relative strengths. Then we simply averaged the components of the four major activities.

7 Note that only descriptive relationships are indicated, and that causal conclusions, such as that networking leads to success, are not warranted in this analysis. Also keep in mind that a sample of 52 RMs, not all the RMs from the four-year study, were used in this "success" part of the study. However, in this part of the analysis, we did add in another sample of 79 RMs from a number of diverse organizations and obtained almost identical results to those shown in Figure 4-2.

Moreover, this finding held no matter how we looked at the data. All three analytic techniques (statistical, comparative, and relative strength of relationship) revealed the same finding: the importance of the networking activity to successful RMs. Our study was crystal clear about the prime importance of networking at every level of analysis: successful RMs do more networking than their less successful counterparts. In addition, we substantiated this finding regardless of the type of organization or the RM's level in the organization. Figure 4-1 showed that successful RMs engage in this activity 70% more than their unsuccessful counterparts, and the relationship analysis shown in Figure 4-2 indicated that networking is almost as strong as the other three activities combined. We will explore this important, but traditionally overlooked, managerial activity more thoroughly in Chapter Seven. In addition, all analyses showed that successful RMs also do relatively more routine communication activities.

Surprisingly, we saw human resource and traditional management activities less frequently in the successful RMs than in the unsuccessful RMs in the comparative analysis, and those activities similarly came out last in the strength of relationship analysis. This finding refutes those who have advocated a human resource management approach and the importance of the traditional management functions. Could it be that successful RMs really give less attention to human resources and traditional management than do their unsuccessful counterparts? Apparently so. This important finding embodies the purpose of this book: discovering empirically, perhaps for the first time, what Real Managers actually do to be successful and effective, and the gap between the prescriptions for success in the management literature and real success.

Let's see what else the numbers tell us. Communication is clearly the second strongest ingredient in RM success: as our comparative analysis indicated, successful RMs engage about 10% more in routine communication activities (exchanging routine information and paperwork) than their unsuccessful counterparts. Furthermore, these findings support what most observers assume to be the importance of communication skills to managerial success. Of course, such skills complement the networking activities of successful RMs.

When we examined the two major behavioral categories in this routine communication activity closely, we found that exchanging routine information accounted for most of the difference between successful and unsuccessful RMs in the comparative analysis. The attention the two groups gave to paperwork was about the same, as shown in both the comparative analysis and the relationship analysis. After the networking activity of socializing/politicking, the communication activity of exchanging routine information had the strongest relationship to success. Handling paperwork, the other communication subcategory, fell in the middle in terms of relative strength of the relationship.

These findings make intuitive sense. Successful RMs are asking for and giving information more often than their unsuccessful counterparts; they are in constant communication with their subordinates. They do the required paperwork, meet deadlines for reports, and cover themselves in a political sense, but the more successful RMs do not make paperwork a top priority. One manager elaborated:

> *I like to keep informed and I like to keep my people informed. Mostly I do this verbally rather than in writing. I prefer to pick up the phone or drop by my people's desks to tell them something or ask them something. I don't write them memos. Unfortunately, that doesn't mean that there is no paperwork in this job. I try to keep up with my inbox and meet all deadlines for reports and requests from the boss. If I don't do at least that much, I look bad, as if I'm letting things slip.*

We found no appreciable difference in communication activities when we analyzed them by type of organization and level in the organization. This matters because it suggests that this kind of routine communication is a universal marker for success, not dependent on the specific situation (such as a specific industry or job level). Like networking, successful RMs in the organizations in our sample, at all levels of these organizations, did more communication activities. Chapter Six discusses the communication activities in more detail.

One of the most striking findings of our study is that successful managers do not seem to be doing nearly as much of the traditional human resources activities as less successful managers. This finding contradicts the behaviorally oriented management literature, which stresses the unqualified importance of human resource management activities. This result was clear in both the comparative analysis and the relative strength of relationship analysis. Successful managers are doing more networking and communication and less human resource management activities. These findings present an interesting and revealing profile of managerial success.

In addition, our findings about human resource activities revealed a key distinction that management literature passes over: the difference between *successful* and *effective* management. The management literature in general, and research in organizational behavior and human resource management in particular, maintains that human resource management activities are necessary specifically for *effective* management, but makes no distinction between success and effectiveness. Yet our findings showed that *successful* RMs are doing relatively less of these activities than their unsuccessful counterparts. Obviously, there are tremendous implications if effective RMs do human resource management activities but successful RMs do not. Chapter Five delves into the profile of *effective* RMs, including the relative importance of human resource management activities to managerial effectiveness, and will explore the implications of the difference between success and effectiveness.

There are several possible explanations why successful RMs give less attention to human resource activities. For example, perhaps successful RMs are more task- or achievement-oriented, an outlook that is incompatible with a human resources approach. It is also possible that a "lag effect," as proposed by pioneering organizational psychologist Rensis Likert, is at work.

Likert argued that the manager who spends a lot of time managing human resources will be more effective, but it takes time (that is, there is a lag) for this to work itself out. The lag stems from the fact that the work unit is managed, over time, by a succession of managers, some of whom take a human resources approach and some who don't. In his survey, Likert found that top management (those making promotions), impatient as they tend to be, often do not let a human resources-oriented manager stay long enough for the lag to take effect. Top management instead brings in an autocratic manager to, as they see it, tighten the ship.[8] This coincides with the effectiveness generated by the previous human resources manager finally taking hold. Thus, the autocratic manager inherits an effective work unit, resulting in a promotion. Or the incoming autocratic manager might exploit the work unit for his or her short-term gain, exiting with a promotion and leaving an ineffective work unit.

The cycle then repeats itself. The autocrat's human resources-oriented successor inherits the ineffective work unit, which takes considerable time to reclaim, reflecting badly on the new manager and impeding his or her chances for promotion—regardless of how much attention is given to the human resources activities. Once managers start to violate the trust of their subordinates, it can take even a human resources-oriented successor considerable time to repair the damage and restore the work unit's effectiveness.

A CLOSER LOOK AT HUMAN RESOURCES
MANAGEMENT ACTIVITIES

Breaking the human resource activity into its component behavioral categories for closer examination revealed some fascinating insights, even more so than when we took a similarly granular look at networking and communicating. One component, managing conflict, was particularly interesting. In the study, we defined this behavior, based on and drawn from direct observation, as:

1. Managing interpersonal conflicts
2. Appealing to higher authority to resolve a dispute
3. Appealing to third-party negotiators
4. Trying to get cooperation or consensus
5. Attempting to resolve conflicts between a subordinate and oneself

Managing conflict was very strongly associated with successful RMs in the comparative analysis and had a moderately strong relationship in the relative strength analysis. A pair of subordinates described successful RMs managing conflict activities in the study:

---

8 What Likert called a Systems I manager.

He often tries to prevent conflict by watching for red flags and then quickly bringing the parties together to come up with a solution before a big fight erupts.

My manager knows how to smooth out conflicts between us. She will listen to both sides and then try to solve the problem so we both think we won.

Further analysis, however, revealed that the managing conflict activity varied considerably with the type of organization and the level of the RM. For example, one of the organizations we studied in depth was a heterogeneous manufacturing plant with many different departments, jobs, people, and profit centers. This variety of power centers meant that the plant was ripe for management conflicts. One manager explained:

We are always competing for resources in this department. I have to spend a lot of my time trying to smooth things out and make sure all the projects meet the deadlines and quality specs. The only way I know how to do this is to act as a mediator and keep things fair for all concerned. Everyone is under pressure and my job is to help interpret the gray areas and keep everybody together for our overall company goals.

Confusion over authority and responsibilities—who controlled their "turf," as some managers in our study put it—plague RMs, especially in the middle- and lower-level ranks. In this organization, successful RMs exhibited considerably more behaviors identified as managing conflict than did their unsuccessful counterparts.

We also studied two organizations in the public sector in this part of the analysis: a state department of revenue and a campus police department. In contrast to the manufacturing plant, formalized structures and hierarchies, as well as mechanistic regulations and control, characterized these public sector organizations. Bureaucratic rules and legal statutes were the norm here. For managers, there was less doubt, less up for grabs, and less likelihood of crossing territorial boundaries—treading on someone else's turf—to get the job done. In both of these public sector organizations, successful RMs exhibited considerably less of the managing conflict human resource activity than did their unsuccessful counterparts. In other words, when the organizational structure clearly defines job roles, particularly in a stable environment, the ability or effort a manager devotes to managing conflict may not lead to success. Conversely, in ill-defined, ambiguous situations, managing conflict may lend itself to success.

In addition to the type of organization, the level of the RM also plays a role in linking conflict management to success. In particular, our analysis indicated that top-level RMs manage conflict much more often than do either mid- or first-level RMs. It may be that top-level RMs are more attentive, or at least sensitive, to dysfunctional conflict and thus give more effort to resolving it. They are more disposed toward peacekeeping. It could also mean that top-level positions tend to be closer to significant territorial disputes because middle- and lower-level RMs, who may work without well-defined rules and boundaries (especially in certain types of organizations), feel this is just part of the job and make no special effort to manage conflict.

So, our study produced at least one remarkable finding about human resource management: managing conflict was closely associated with success, but only in certain situations. What about the other human resources behaviors? Here again, we found something extraordinary: successful RMs, in general, don't do human resources—except for the special cases of conflict management we just detailed. Indeed, the relative lack of human resource management activities done by successful RMs is one of the most important findings in our study, and we will continue to probe its implications for organizational effectiveness and subordinate productivity throughout the rest of the book. Here are the topline details: In the comparative analysis, we found that training/developing was done equally by successful and unsuccessful managers. However, motivating/reinforcing was done a surprising 30% less by successful RMs, and staffing was done a whopping 70% less by successful RMs. In the relative strength of relationship analysis, motivating/reinforcing had a moderately strong relationship, but, echoing the comparative analysis, both staffing and training/developing had a very weak relationship to success. Unlike managing conflict, neither the type of organization nor the level of the RM affected these results.

Again, keep in mind that the analyses do not indicate causal relationships. For example, the very weak showing of the staffing activity could be attributed to successful RMs being so efficiently organized that they do not have to reconfigure or reschedule very often. It may also be that turnover and absenteeism are low, their subordinates may get to work on time, and successful RMs may not need to find replacements very often. If someone should quit or be absent, there may be contingency plans to handle the load or predetermined work priorities that permit some work to be deferred until the vacancy is filled. Less successful managers may lack the freedom or the ability to make such plans or priorities.

The latter type of manager may also create high rates of turnover, absenteeism, and tardiness. For example, when the manager doesn't realistically plan vacations into the schedule, employees in many work units are expected to finish the work left undone during their time off. Conversely, planning for short-run personnel shortages, such as allowing for absentees, justifiable lateness, or vacations reduces ambiguity and job stress. Realistic staffing makes subordinates happier and reduces turnover, absenteeism, and tardiness. When these positive trends are happening at the same time, a sense of fairness prevails that may reduce the staffing requirements for successful RMs.

The more obvious explanation for the marked dearth of human resource management activities among successful RMs, of course, is simply that they don't do them—or, at least, they do relatively less of them. We will continue to pursue this line of inquiry, and its implications for organizational effectiveness and subordinate satisfaction, throughout this book.

TRADITIONAL MANAGEMENT ACTIVITIES OF SUCCESSFUL RMS

Traditional management activities—decision-making, planning, and controlling—had even less impact on RM success than human resources activities. As Figure 4-1 showed, traditional management activities fared even worse than human resource management activities in the comparative analysis. Successful RMs did 40% less of these activities than did their unsuccessful counterparts. Also, on the relative strength of relationship analysis, Figure 4-2 shows that traditional management activities were very close to human resource management activities for the weakest relationships to managerial success. Let's examine each of these activities in turn.

Decision-Making

Contrary to the portrait drawn in textbooks and business classes, Real Managers do not make glamorous economic decisions or determine the fate of multinational conglomerates. Nor do they usually decide whether their organization will attempt a stock takeover of another corporation, determine how to defend themselves against a hostile takeover, or set overall corporate strategy and policy. Management literature overemphasizes the traditional management activity of decision-making. We found it to be much narrower in scope and importance for our successful RMs than scholars—and managers themselves—tend to find. Instead, Real Managers make many modest or even insignificant decisions that are nevertheless essential to daily, weekly, and monthly operations of their areas of responsibility.

Even though companies deem the decision-making activity to be important, our comparative analysis found that the most successful of the RMs devoted about the same effort to making decisions as did the least successful did. The relative strength of relationship analysis found decision-making even less dominant than the comparative analysis. Only planning and the human resource management activities had weaker relationships to success. Although the type of organization does not seem to matter, as in the managing conflict activity, our analysis revealed that the relationship of decision-making to successful managers did seem to depend on the level of the RM.

As you would expect, decision-making opportunities and authority graduate by level, increasing as the manager moves upward in the organizational hierarchy. At least on this activity, a traditional management perspective may be at work. At lower levels, formalization and structure (through rules and regulations) can reduce the manager's decision-making opportunities drastically. Further analysis revealed that top-level RMs do much more decision-making than do mid- or first-level RMs. This indicates that bureaucratic hierarchy and chain-of-command authority limit the amount of decision-making possible. Top-level RMs have more decision-making_*opportunities* than RMs at lower levels: as a step function, the difference in decision-making opportunities changes sharply, rather than gradually, in each step of the hierarchy.

At top-level management, where the work is less routine, decisions must be made more often. Organizations reduce lower-level decision-making through bureaucratic policies, rules and regulations, and computerization. One manager commented:

Sure, I would like to be able to make more decisions and solve problems to show my boss that I am executive material. But in this job, I have very little discretion. I have to go by what the numbers say or by existing policy handed down to me. I seldom have a chance to make a decision.

Conventional wisdom gives much attention to decision-making; in fact, it's sometimes even equated with management. Even though this may be true for top-level management, RMs at lower levels, like the manager quoted above, just don't have as much of a chance to exercise their decision-making skills, and, more importantly, do not generally feel empowered to make decisions anyway. Chapter Five will give more detailed attention to decision-making and other dimensions of the traditional management activities of RMs.

Planning and Success

In the comparative analysis, we observed that more successful RMs did less planning than their unsuccessful counterparts. However, planning had the weakest relationship to success of all the activities we studied. Once again, the type of organization seems to make little difference, but, as in the decision-making finding, when success was defined as the RM reaching the top level of management, we found that such RMs do much more planning than mid-level or first-level RMs. This analysis, in other words, supports traditional notions about the importance of planning, at least for top-level executives. Nevertheless, the overall findings provide several interesting insights into the question of what successful RMs do.

First, the traditional management literature doesn't consider whether some functions—planning, for example—are more or less important at different levels of management. This literature tends to focus on top management, but it implies that its maxims about strategic planning are universal truths applicable to all levels. This is, we discovered, an oversimplification. Second, our resource suggests that, because of external forces like the economy or technological change, many organizations have moved to centralize the planning function, which leaves less opportunity for planning at lower levels.

Third, we found out what less successful managers are not doing when they spend too much time planning. Unlike their more successful counterparts who plan judiciously, less successful managers engage in planning activities at the expense of other important activities that would have a much greater impact on their potential success, especially networking and communicating activities. A subordinate described an unsuccessful manager's planning activity this way:

> *He always has us busy inputting into the long-range plan for the department. He seems to be spinning his wheels in this regard. However, his counterpart over in the sales department seems conveniently to ignore the long-range plan and is busy politicking with the boss for more resources and keeping his people informed on a daily basis.*

This is a stark illustration of stuck-in-the-mud planning; not just because the manager was wasting time on unnecessary long-range planning, but also because his unfortunate team could see much different results one department away. Furthermore, the sales manager was probably not "ignoring" the long-range plan—she just had it in the proper perspective.

Fourth, our study revealed that planning is a skill that is not equally developed among all managers. This means that the frequency of planning, or even simply the amount of time spent at it, doesn't necessarily distinguish the successful from the less successful manager. Well-honed talent and keen insight matter, too; in other words, a manager who is simply not any good at it can plan until kingdom come without it having much effect, if any. The quality of a plan lies in whether it can feasibly and efficiently be translated and executed into bottom-line results, and RMs with a well-developed planning sense can forge the link between idea and execution with relative ease. Less successful managers spend more time preparing ineffective plans, planning the wrong things, or substituting plans for real action and performance (like the first manager in the example from the last paragraph).

Finally, less successful RMs may be spending more time planning in order to overprotect themselves, whether it's to evade responsibility for failures, because they lack confidence in their subordinates, or some other reason. If things go wrong because of an unwillingness to delegate and empower subordinates to effectively execute the plan, the manager can point to his well-thought-out plan and blame the subordinates for their deficiencies in being able to carry it out. This kind of manager, I think we can all agree, is *prima facie* on the road to ineffectiveness and lack of success.

Controlling and Success

Managers control. They make sure goals and plans are being carried out through behaviors like inspecting work, walking around and checking things out, and monitoring performance data (all specific categories of controlling we used). In our study, the traditional management activity of controlling fared even worse than decision-making and planning in the comparative success analysis, but better in the relative strength of relationship analysis. The top third of successful RMs were observed to engage in controlling much less than the bottom third of unsuccessful RMs, but the relative strength of the relationship of this activity to success put it in the middle of all the managerial activities. Again, the type of organization does not seem to matter, but when success was defined as reaching the top level of management, we found that these top-level managers control less than those at the middle and first levels.

This may seem confusing at first; it sounds like controlling activities are related to success, yet too much controlling is not a successful behavior. How can this be? The traditional perspective, of course, is that performing the control function is an activity that is central to a manager's success. Our result, confusing on the surface, actually reveals something quite profound: the efficiency of the method of control may be more important than how much a manager is directly involved in the process of control. We would certainly not argue against the contribution the control activity can make to managerial success, but what matters is the quality, not the quantity, of control. In particular, we found that:

1. *Top-level RMs find the right level of control.* More successful RMs, especially those at upper levels of the hierarchy, seem to reach an optimum level of controlling performance and stop there; beyond this optimum level, more control is wasted effort. Successful RMs may be able to adjust the amount of personal control required of them by altering the organization's control systems and work environments. They do this by influencing their superiors, maintaining effective relationships with subordinates, developing consistency (even routinizing change), delegating, and distributing written policies and procedures. These activities complement the successful manager's networking and communicating activities and help RMs stabilize their work environments. Such approaches accomplish more control with less direct effort and free managers for other important activities.

2. *The control activity is a high-risk function.* Because success depends on other people (as evidenced by the importance of networking), the RM whose performance is more dependent on controlling the performance of others may be at greater risk of failure than the RM whose performance is less dependent on others. Control can be a negative experience; a Real Manager who must devote a lot of time and effort to it because of the nature of the job or because of style may not win many friends or influence the powerful people necessary for success.

The disconnect between what the management literature says successful managers should do and what successful Real Managers actually do is startling. As we have seen, successful RMs concentrate on networking and, to a lesser degree, communicating activities. But, contrary to management gurus, successful managers do not do as much human resource management and traditional management activities as their unsuccessful counterparts. And these are not the only ways that reality belies assumptions about what makes a successful manager. These assumptions have been hardened by decades of being taken at face value, but in many cases, they don't reflect reality.

They have, in fact, become myths. Let's reexamine some of the myths surrounding managerial success.

THE MYTH OF SHARED PSYCHOLOGICAL CHARACTERISTICS

One school of thought in management literature suggests that successful managers share common psychological characteristics like:

1. A strong need to achieve
2. A strong need to obtain and use power
3. A relatively weak need for affiliation
4. Complex reasoning patterns and the ability to process lots of information
5. Relatively high intelligence

Although some successful managers undoubtedly have these characteristics, there has been no evidence to date to suggest that *successful* managers possess them in greater (or lesser) amounts than unsuccessful managers.[9] Presumably, all good managers have a strong need to achieve. However, the motivation of high achievement can be situational specific when it comes to managerial success. For example, in many highly structured public service jobs, managers can rise to high-level positions without a strong need to achieve (for example, they can be successful through a political payoff). The desire to achieve, which outsiders or organizations might see as grasping, can even backfire: it's conceivable that by demonstrating unusual achievement motivation, a manager might be regarded as a threat to their contemporaries, superiors, or "the system," resulting in career failure, rather than career success.

One of our Real Managers fit this description. His ambition was to retire on a small farm on the southern Pacific coast and to supplement his retirement income with income from the farm. He was an upper-level manager whose primary job was to locate and acquire essential new equipment for a very large federal agency operating in an unstable environment. His purview included budgets of hundreds of millions of dollars. Before assuming this high-responsibility job, he had performed

---

9 Famed Harvard psychologist David McClelland conducted research relating the drive for achievement and power to effective managers.

routine duties for his entire 27-year career in the civil service. He was elevated to his current position—in his own assessment as well as that of others who knew him—on the strength of his benign personality (he was "well liked"). This position had historically been a final stepping-stone to top-level management and was usually reserved for entrepreneurial managers with extraordinarily strong needs to achieve and to distinguish themselves. However, this RM did not fit the mold: he operated in a "caretaker" role until he quietly retired three years later.

Here is a case in which top-level management had decided that they could afford to sacrifice a position to marginal productivity in order to provide a holding area for a mediocre senior manager until he retired. In fact, this RM was selected because he was not a threat to the manager one level above (who had himself been assigned as a consequence of failure in his previous job). The point is not that there is no justice or logic to managerial success, nor that what makes a manager successful is beyond understanding, but that we may be thinking of success in inappropriate—or overly logical—ways.

It is easy to dismiss the analysis of success in this example as being typical of government jobs but not of business and industry standards of success. Yet doesn't the same thing happen in organizations in the private sector, where there is often no clear accountability for performance? We found many successful RMs who seemed to defy traditional ideas about what psychological traits are needed for managerial success.

THE MYTH THAT SUBORDINATE SATISFACTION RELATES TO MANAGERIAL SUCCESS

Another school of management literature suggests that managerial success is based on subordinate satisfaction and organizational commitment. The theory is that managers influence their subordinates' satisfaction and acceptance of organizational goals and values, which in turn influences work unit performance. According to conventional wisdom, all of this will lead to the success of the manager. Evidence suggests that satisfied employees who are also committed and loyal to their organizational goals are more likely to be productive than employees who are dissatisfied and not committed to those goals. But is manager *success* actually related to subordinate satisfaction and commitment? We did not find evidence to support this assumption. This is a prime example of management experts confusing success with effectiveness; subordinate commitment may very well engender effective work units and organizations, but our study couldn't link it to the success of individual RMs.

THE MYTH OF STEADY WORK

The adage instructs, "Keep your eye on the ball, your shoulder to the wheel, your nose to the grindstone, and your ear to the ground, and you will be successful." Could anyone really work in such a position? Which of these bits of sage advice are to be believed, and in what order?

Traditional management literature and classic theories lay down some specific guidelines to be a successful manager. For example, we noted in Chapter Two that the "father" of the functional/process approach to management, Henri Fayol, prescribed a five-step approach to success: plan, organize, command, coordinate, and control. Other classical management theorists, such as Luther Gulick, recommended seven ingredients of success: plan, organize, staff, direct, coordinate, report, and budget. Other classical writers, such as Lyndall Urwick, have suggested as many as 29 such ingredients. Every management function that has ever been conceived undoubtedly has a proponent somewhere.

If we consider all the prescriptions for manager success, we see that not very much is really known about the subject. If we aggregated all of them, we might arrive at "Work very hard." In fact, the end result verges on a sort of tautology: "Be successful by being successful." Many of these traditional prescriptions appear to be only general guidelines, sometimes subject to serious error when they are followed. We found many successful departures from the classical prescriptions (for example, one successful manager came up through project engineering in an environment where most of the classical prescriptions were violated dramatically).

The traditional behavioral prescriptions include such ingredients as team building, goal setting, coaching, facilitating, and participating. These are merely representative, and experts tend to acknowledge them in a general way rather than directly linking them to managerial success. We have examined more than 130 of these factors in our research. We found that many of them relate to many things, but few relate directly to the success of the RMs we studied.

Our study provides pragmatic advice and guidance for those who want to get ahead and climb the ladder of success in today's organizations. One thing in particular stands out in sharp relief: Networking and communication skills are the keys to success. Honing these skills will do more than anything else we know of to move a manager up the management hierarchy—to make them successful. But, as we found from our study of RMs and have repeatedly stressed, *successful* is not the same thing as *effective*. Therefore, we now turn to that other key question for today's thoughtful managers: What do *effective* Real Managers do?

CHAPTER **FIVE**
Effective Managers

*It seems that no matter how hard I work, I can't seem
to get ahead in this company. Sure, I get a pat on
the back once in a while and I'm assured a secure
position. But the smooth talkers, not the hard workers,
seem to move into top management around here. It's
very frustrating to me to work my tail off on a project,
involve my people, and make sure it's done right,
when I know it may not be as important as my golf
game and being able to talk sports with the boss.*

"**S**UCCESSFUL" AND "EFFECTIVE" ARE NOT INTERCHANGEABLE
terms. Managers who are effective (those who have satisfied, committed subordinates and produce organizational results) are not necessarily those who succeed (those who are promoted relatively quickly).
Managers know that such disparities exist, and many, including the
Real Manager quoted above, suspect that the disconnect between success and effectiveness is quite common. Our study of RMs *proves* this
to be the rule, rather than the exception. Successful RMs and effective
RMs engage in different amounts and types of managerial activities.
Therefore, our study raises a question central to modern management:
How can a Real Manager be successful and effective at the same time?
We will return to this central question again, but first we have to examine managerial effectiveness, and what it means.

Starting with the scientific management movement at the turn of the
20th century, managerial effectiveness focused on getting the job done,
in the most direct, efficient way. It mainly recommended a task-oriented
approach as the key to effective management. Thus, managers equated
organizational effectiveness, stressing quantity and quality standards of

performance, with managerial effectiveness. More recently, management wisdom has also advocated a more humanistic approach, which links employee satisfaction and commitment with managerial effectiveness.

Management practitioners, writers, researchers, and even lay-people, tend to view successful managers and effective managers as the same and use the terms "successful" and "effective" interchangeably, but the difference may be vital to explaining the current state of American management. If indeed we can empirically demonstrate the difference between successful RMs and effective RMs, we can explain past problems and how American organizations can gain a competitive advantage in the global economy instead of relying too heavily on advanced technology and information systems. Even more critical, we might address the growing frustration and deteriorating confidence that hard-working, effective RMs seem to be experiencing in recent times.

This important distinction between effectiveness and success may be crucial to the understanding and practice of modern management. And management literature has almost totally ignored this key divide—until now.

What do effective RMs do? This is the most important question we address, because it represents the bottom line for managers and their organizations. By the same token, it's the most difficult to answer, because of the problems of defining effectiveness, trying to measure it in RMs in different organizations, and drawing meaningful conclusions from complex data. It will help to begin by summarizing how effective managers have been portrayed in the traditional literature, which will help us understand the significance of the gap between successful and effective RMs. The consequences of that gap on the day-to-day lives of managers will become apparent when we delve into the results of our study: in other words, the background and results of the third phase of our analysis that gets to the heart of what effective Real Managers do.

Like they have in the literature on activities of managers in general and successful managers in particular, much of the management theory in print about effective managers and effective managing is prescriptive: "what to do" to become an effective manager, or worse, "what to be." Managers reading the collection of "should-do," "should-be" prescriptions are sure to find that they are not following, and probably cannot follow, all or even most of them.

Table 5-1 shows a representative sample of no fewer than 50 prescriptions for effective managers that we extracted from the considerable literature on the subject.

TABLE 5-1
Prescriptions for Effectiveness
Drawn from Management Literature

1. Be proactive—initiate—anticipate	26. Emphasize goals
2. Control your time	27. Encourage action
3. Be the leader	28. Facilitate interaction among participants
4. Control your decision-making groups	29. Facilitate work
5. Don't over-control	30. Be attentive to product quality
6. Don't under-control	31. Arrange a clean, pleasant physical work environment
7. Communicate	32. Develop yourself
8. Don't get into trouble from communicating too much	33. Develop your subordinates
9. Keep your organization open with a high level of trust	34. Motivate
10. Take time to reflect on problems and solutions	35. Build up your subordinates
11. Seek help when you need it	36. Make your subordinates want to come to work
12. Let the experts do their jobs	37. Be patient
13. Be assertive	38. Be sincere
14. Renegotiate your job if you have to	39. Recognize good work
15. Protect yourself	40. Reward fairly
16. Choose appropriate objectives	41. Don't demand performance from high performers
17. Be accurate	42. Do demand performance from low performers
18. Set realistic goals	43. Control poor work
19. Know the objectives	44. Terminate non-workers
20. Choose the right people for effectiveness	45. Properly deal with inspectors
21. Match jobs and people	46. Carefully build and control your budget
22. Design your organization for effectiveness	47. Keep good records
23. Design the jobs for effectiveness	48. Participate in the community
24. Create a supportive environment to get the job done	49. Make it fun
25. Encourage attitudes to improve productivity	50. Innovate—make positive changes

Who can argue against these prescriptions? Most managers are trying, with varying results, to do these kinds of things, but no manager can effectively go in 50 or more directions at the same time. Are the prescriptions of equal importance? How much effort should be applied to what, and when should it be applied? Some RM activities take less effort and contribute more, or are more closely related to effectiveness measures, than others. If these activities could be prioritized, or weighed in order of importance, RMs could better analyze their own strengths and weaknesses and systematically develop the most important activities first.

Measuring manager effectiveness, a seemingly simple task, can become hopelessly complex. We described in Chapter Two how we approached this conundrum: We gathered data from the focused sample of 52 RMs from a narrower group of organizations, and we cast our net wider to encompass a larger sample of 178 RMs from a broad range of industries. The context for our tightly focused study is the vast and unmanageable number of managerial effectiveness or performance measures we found in a survey of the literature. Table 5-2 shows some of these—more than 2,000 of them!

TABLE 5-2
Sample Number of Available Measures of Manager Effectiveness

Production	252	Materials Handling	93
Sales	199	Maintenance	91
Comptroller	180	Production Planning	83
Marketing	172	Treasurer	81
Personnel	169	Research and Development	76
Facilities/Plant	144	Quality Assurance	66
Purchasing	125	Data Processing/Management Information Systems	65
Manufacturing/Industrial Engineering	102	General Effectiveness	44
		Total	**1,942**

Obviously, 2,000 or even 44 measures (the smallest number shown), are far too many to evaluate in a study of manager effectiveness. That's why we built our study around the same four activities of *successful* RMs we discussed in the last chapter—communication, human resource management, traditional management, and networking. Later in this chapter, we will show the relative weight of these four activities for *effective* RMs. We based our conclusions both on direct observation of RMs and on standardized questionnaires asking subordinates how they view the effectiveness of their managers. Our intent was not to urge RMs to do impression management (that is, managing impressions about their effectiveness) as a substitute for getting the job done. Nor did we want to replace hard measures like quality, service, productivity rates, and profits. Rather, studies like ours, with its dual-sourced methodologies (observers and subordinates, in this case) and its perceptions and impressions of manager effectiveness, have been demonstrated to be reliable and valid enough to draw meaningful conclusions about what effective RMs do. In the end, we wanted to get at questions of effectiveness empirically, in order to cut the Gordian knot of what makes an effective manager—a knot tangled up in thousands of measures that are supposed to gauge effectiveness. What did we find?

We'll make it very clear right off the bat: communication and human resource management are the keys. Here's how we got there. To directly compare the *successful* RMs with the *effective* RMs, we first used the same sample of 52 RMs used in the success analysis of Chapter Three. However, to gauge effectiveness, we combined subordinate satisfaction and commitment only; the organizational unit performance measure used in the rest of the analysis was not available to us on this sample of 52 RMs. The results are shown in Figure 5-1. Notice that there are some distinct differences between the relative contributions of the four RM activities to success and effectiveness (defined in this case as subordinate satisfaction and commitment) using the *same sample*. In particular, note the reversed roles of networking (strongest for success, weakest for effectiveness) and human resource management (second strongest for effectiveness, weakest for success).

FIGURE 5-1

Comparison of the Contributions of RM Activities to Effectiveness and Success

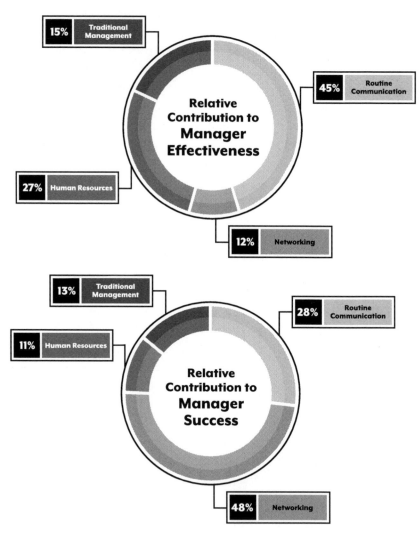

To do a more comprehensive, fully descriptive treatment of RM effectiveness, we went beyond the sample of 52 managers used in the success part of the study and analyzed 178 RMs and their direct subordinates (an average of about four subordinates each). We used correlations between the directly observed behaviors of the 178 RMs'

activities and the combined effectiveness measure, which included the organizational unit performance scale as well as the subordinate satisfaction and commitment scales. Figure 5-2 shows the relative strengths of the contributions of the four major activities to effectiveness. Notice that these proportions of activities drawn from this large sample (N = 178 RMs) are almost identical to the smaller sample (N = 52 RMs) used in Figure 5-1. In other words, for both the small and large samples, we got the same results: networking had the strongest relative relationship to success and the weakest to effectiveness; and human resource management had a solid relationship to effectiveness (second strongest) and the weakest to success. Communication showed the strongest relationship to effectiveness, followed by human resource management.

FIGURE 5-2
Contribution to Manager Effectiveness
(using analysis of 178 RMs and their subordinates)

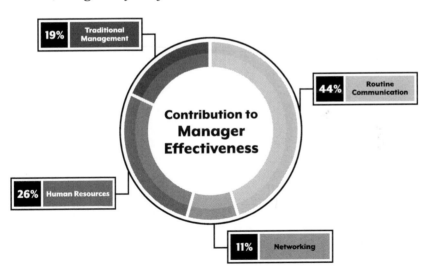

COMMUNICATION ACTIVITIES OF EFFECTIVE RMS

We were not surprised by the importance of communication to effectiveness, even though traditional management theory has ignored it (for example, it is not one of Fayol's five famous functions of management). The field of communication studies has emphasized the importance of communication activities to managers through the years, and common sense tells us that lack of communication can grind organizations to a halt. But what kinds of communication are the most effective? Perhaps surprisingly, it turns out that many of the routine, unremarkable behaviors of day-to-day communication grease the wheels better than anything—that is, they are related most strongly to effectiveness. Communication was associated with effectiveness in exchanging routine information behaviors such as:

- Answering routine procedural questions
- Receiving and disseminating requested information
- Conveying the results of meetings
- Giving or receiving routine information over the phone
- Attending informational staff meetings

Communication was also tied to effectiveness in paperwork-handling behaviors, including:

- Processing mail
- Reading reports
- Emptying the inbox
- Writing reports, memos, and letters
- Routine financial reporting and bookkeeping
- General desk work

Astonishingly, exchanging routine information had the highest relative strength of relationship to effectiveness, and processing paperwork had the second highest of all the managerial behaviors observed in the study. Anecdotally, the managers in our study backed up the relative importance of these seemingly mundane activities. One commented:

> I'll have to admit that the secret to getting things done in my department and keeping my people happy is simply to keep them informed. I constantly get on the phone to them or stop by their desks to tell them or ask them what's going on. I also keep up with my paperwork and meet all my report deadlines.

It seems that persistently focusing on the routines of email, paper-work, and everyday face-to-face communication is one of the keys to being an effective manager. This is not to say that these things are the be-all, end-all of effective management, nor does it mean that just doing them is enough—it's still possible to do them poorly. It does mean, however, that honing one's skills in these small, daily transac-tions can add up to something big.

Because communication activities were so strongly related to RM effectiveness, we also analyzed *how* RMs communicate. We asked a sample of 120 RMs from a small number of diverse organizations to fill out a questionnaire reporting their communication behaviors. Figure 5-3 shows that almost half of their self-reported communication was with subordinates. They distributed the remainder among others out-side the organization (about one fourth), others inside the organiza-tion (about one fifth), and, least of all, with their bosses (about 15%). In addition, they reported that most of their communication, by far, was on an informal face-to-face basis.

FIGURE 5-3
RMs Communicate With...

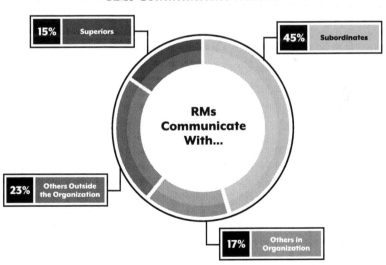

A word about modern electronic communication: we should note that these data were gathered before the era of email, smartphones, and sophisticated information systems dependent on broadband internet. However, a follow-up study after 15 years of over 300 tech-savvy managers from a wide variety of functions and organizations (using the same basic framework as our original study) got similar results. The only difference was they spent a little less time on routine communication and a little more on human resources, presumably because automated information systems in place freed them up to spend more time on their people.[10] We will explore communication activities in considerable detail in Chapter Six.

HUMAN RESOURCE ACTIVITIES OF EFFECTIVE RMS

After communication, nothing contributed more, relatively, to RM effectiveness than human resource management activity. This crucial finding supports management literature for both researchers and practitioners, much of which has long argued for the importance of human resources and humanistic, positive approaches to management. But none of this literature tells the whole story. The practitioner-oriented literature usually supports its positions and recommendations on individual cases, intuition, and interesting, lively writing, while the research-oriented literature relies on questionnaire survey data or unrealistic laboratory studies. By using a data-driven approach supplemented with anecdotal examples, our observational study completed the picture and made the importance of human resource management activities for effective performance really stand out in sharp relief. One manager elaborated on the human resource activity as follows:

> *I know how to handle my people. I don't let things fester.*
> *When any of my people have a grievance, they know that*
> *we can settle it together. They know where they stand, and*
> *what I expect. I take a hard line on bickering—just don't*
> *tolerate it, but I always recognize and reward good work.*
> *I make sure that everyone who works for me knows his*

10 Asllani, A. & Luthans, F. (2003) What knowledge managers really do: an empirical and comparative analysis. *Journal of Knowledge Management,* 7(3), 53-66.

job. We operate like a big family in my department. I have good people working for me, and I back them to the hilt. They know I care, but I'm not a busybody or a "softy." Once in a great while, I have someone who can't carry responsibility for his own work. Then I have to replace him. I don't like it, but in the long run, it saves me and everyone else in the department a lot of grief. Caring about my people works. These guys really produce when you need them.

This manager's story demonstrates the kind of flexible human relationships that tend to go hand in hand with effective management.

Beyond anecdotal evidence, however, our study measured a strong relationship between human resource management activities and RM effectiveness. This measurable effect was noticeable to an extent in each category of human resource management activity. These include:

- *Managing conflict behaviors:*
  - Resolving interpersonal conflict among subordinates or others
  - Appealing to higher authority or to third-party negotiators to resolve a dispute
  - Trying to get cooperation or consensus among conflicting parties
  - Attempting to resolve conflicts between subordinates and oneself
- *Staffing behaviors:*
  - Developing job descriptions for position openings
  - Reviewing applications
  - Interviewing applicants
  - Hiring
  - Informing applicants of hiring decisions
  - Filling in where needed
- *Training and developing behaviors:*
  - Orienting employees
  - Arranging training seminars
  - Clarifying roles, duties, and job descriptions
  - Coaching, mentoring, and doing task walk-throughs
  - Helping subordinates with personal development plans

- *Motivating/reinforcing behaviors:*
  - Allocating formal organizational rewards
  - Soliciting input and participation
  - Conveying appreciation and compliments
  - Giving due credit
  - Listening to suggestions
  - Giving positive performance feedback
  - Increasing job challenge
  - Delegating responsibility and authority
  - Letting subordinates determine how to do their own work
  - Sticking up for the group to superiors and others
  - Backing a subordinate

Managing conflict behaviors had the strongest relationship to effectiveness, followed closely by staffing behaviors and training/developing behaviors. Motivating/reinforcing behaviors was last, but still had a measurable and important relationship to effectiveness.

These human resource management behaviors are more personalized than the ones associated with traditional management activities. Their strong relationship to effectiveness empirically demonstrates that the human resources approach contributes significantly to RM effectiveness. It's important to note as well that the observable behaviors that make up these activities clearly illustrate that a human-oriented approach does not erode the RM's formal power and authority to get the job done. On the contrary, Real Managers can strengthen and increase their bases of power using a human resources approach and reap the results on the bottom line.

TRADITIONAL MANAGEMENT ACTIVITIES OF EFFECTIVE RMS

Traditional management activities—decision-making, planning, and controlling—ranked third out of four in their relative contribution to RMs' effectiveness. Most interesting, decision-making related the least of the three to effectiveness. This was a surprising result, since these behaviors (which include defining problems; choosing between two or more alternatives or strategies; handling day-to-day operational crises as they arise; weighing trade-offs and doing cost/benefit analysis; developing new procedures to increase efficiency; and actually deciding what to do) are so often emphasized as effective management. Indeed, as we indicated in our discussion of successful managers, American business education tends to *equate* good management with decisive decision-making.

It may be that today's organizations, with their emphasis on strategic decision-making, have moved this function exclusively to top-level management and have left out the typical RM. The planning and controlling behaviors remain relevant to RMs, but most formal decision-making has moved steadily upward in American business organizations. This observation squares with some of our interviews and interactions with RMs. As one manager noted:

> *The key to doing well and getting the job done around here is to be organized and to stay on top of things. Staying on top of things is a full-time job. For example, we're just getting computers online in some of our major service areas. They'll help us to organize and control our work better and give us more time for long-range planning and innovation. Up till now, only the front office has had computer capabilities, so we had to rely on them to do our planning and controlling for us down here. They made all of the decisions and we had to implement them. We hope that is now going to change.*

This manager lamented the lack of a role in strategic decision-making, even while identifying a seemingly significant role as an innovator. His organization seemed to still be working out roles in the midst of a long-standing mode of top-level decision-making.

The controlling behaviors (inspecting work; walking around; monitoring performance data such as computer printouts, production, or financial reports; and doing preventive maintenance) related more closely to effectiveness than did decision-making. Planning behaviors (such as setting goals and objectives; defining necessary tasks to accomplish goals; scheduling employees and making timetables; assigning tasks and giving routine instructions; coordinating activities of different subordinates and groups to keep work running smoothly; and organizing the work) ran a close second.

NETWORKING ACTIVITIES OF EFFECTIVE RMS

Networking activities had the weakest relationship to RM effectiveness. This, of course, is in stark contrast to its relationship to RM *success* where it had—by far—the strongest relationship. Of the two component behavioral categories that make up networking, the interacting with outsiders (doing public relations; contacting customers, suppliers, and vendors; attending external meetings; and doing community service activities) was more strongly related to effectiveness than socializing/politicking (network-related chitchat; talking about family or personal matters; informal joking around; discussing rumors, hearsay, and the grapevine; complaining, griping, and downgrading others; and politicking and gamesmanship).

The findings of the success and effectiveness analyses indicate that RMs' networking activities are a way to get ahead in an organization but have little to do with effective day-to-day management. In other words, those RMs who are being promoted (that is, successful RMs) are good at and pay a lot of attention to social and political skills, but are not necessarily the most effective managers. Effective RMs are instead those who give relatively more attention to the other activities, especially communicating and human resource management. Of course, this isn't true in every case—there are some RMs who are both successful *and* effective (more on this in Chapter Nine)—but our study clearly revealed a gap between the two when we drilled down to specific behaviors. And at the same time, our close, detailed look uncovered some of the myths associated with the many prescriptions for and measures of managerial effectiveness that we started this chapter with. Just as we did with success, let's try to debunk a few of the myths of effectiveness.

MYTHS OF EFFECTIVENESS

Take a quick glance back at Tables 5-1 and 5-2 (and try not to start banging your head against the nearest wall). Those 50 prescriptions and the approximately 2,000 available measures of managerial effectiveness that bewilder RMs instead of making their job easier, are a managerial puzzle that needs to be reduced to basics. The prescriptions in Table 5-1 all focused on ways for the RM to control specific results. Trying to put the focus back on interactions between people, we defined RM effectiveness in terms of influencing others in their environments (including subordinates, peers, and bosses) in order to get their jobs done. This involves earning the trust of the people they must influence, and trust connotes a reputation for predictability and fairness. This is always a difficult goal, and it's impossible for the non-communicative, non-human-oriented manager. This is precisely what our observations of RMs showed: the most effective RMs do more communicating and human resource management activities than those who are less effective.

How does this explode myths of managerial effectiveness? When Henri Fayol laid down his principles of management in the early part of the 20th century, the economic, legal, and cultural environments favored managers. Although their freedom was shrinking, they still had the power to run their organizations like feudal baronies (and some managers still do). They could employ at will. They could freely set working hours, compensation, and performance standards. Although standards for sheer physical effort (long working hours, heavy lifting, and so forth) were higher than today, overall productivity was low by today's standards, because mechanized, automated, and robotic production was nonexistent or still in its infancy. The environment external to the organization was more stable. Consequently, the organization, the work, and manager/worker expectations changed slowly. The world today, with its multifarious markets, organizations, jobs, tasks, and expectations regarding pay, promotion, and treatment, is far more uncertain and dynamic. Although these changes don't signal the fall of all the traditional approaches to management, they do herald a need to reexamine *how* managers implement those traditional approaches. When we find something that we think works, we stay with it—often to the exclusion of something better.

Take planning, for example. It is common for RMs trained as functional specialists (for example, accounting, finance, operations research, or even human resources) to identify their success with this technical aspect of their career, especially if they spent their formative years working as technicians in their specialties. The result is that when they move into positions involving more interaction with subordinates, they will probably retain the habits of concentration and the need for isolation and privacy that were essential in their earlier technical experiences (and successes).

The same can be said for the organizing function. This area usually focuses on organizing data, events, materials, and processes, and structuring the organization. Here again, specialists can progress early in their careers, oblivious to the many implications their work has for trust, subordinate commitment and satisfaction, and, most importantly, the effects they can and do have on their people and the effectiveness of the unit.

In the staffing function, RMs are often confronted with a catch-22: No one wants to reward weak performers or overlook strong performers. Nevertheless, RMs in the staffing function often do just that: they allocate more resources to the weakest performers. The weakest performers receive extra training, extra attention, and occasionally even extra rewards (particularly when performance is impossible to measure objectively or when "improvement in performance" measures are used). At best, many HR systems simply fail to distinguish performance differences through recognition and reward systems. We were amazed at the number of experienced RMs who, over time, seemed to develop a blind spot to this issue.

A case in point was one organization we found with 300 employees and a performance recognition program founded on one employee of the month for the entire organization (the likelihood of being recognized was less than once in 25 years). A second case was a large organization with serious performance problems and high waste rates, involving complex processes with new technology. Their product was unusually sensitive to the quality of worker input. When we asked about the options available to reward outstanding performance, the RM shrugged and said, "They get their paychecks." With more than 20 years of field experience, this manager was a product of the traditional management school. He was honest and dedicated to hard work. But his subordinates, with experiences different from his own, had different performance-reward expectations.

Sometimes, RMs can't avoid these upside-down reward systems. In the long run, however, differential rewards based on differential performance become necessary for effective performance. When managers pursue the traditional prescriptions for effectiveness on the basis of technical adequacy without regard to their effects on subordinate attitudes and performance, those prescriptions become myths.

Traditional management principles remain important, but they need a catalyst to translate them from myth to reality. That catalyst—giving priority to communicating and human resources activities—is at the core of RM effectiveness. Spending time doing and perfecting communication and human resources activities and filtering them through traditional management processes makes outcomes predictable for workers: they are able to predict those outcomes based on their own performance. Effective and predictable management, whether in training and developing, motivating and reinforcing, or anything else, helps workers trust the organization and results in high unit performance and subordinate satisfaction and commitment. This doesn't imply that communication and human resource management are the only ingredients necessary for effectiveness. It does suggest that for the most effective RMs, communicating and human resource management activities are an *integral part* of their jobs, and thus their contribution to organizational effectiveness. Less effective managers deal with the human component by ignoring or fragmenting it, often leaving it to other functional specialists and technicians.

In many ways, the question asked in this chapter—What do effective RMs do?—is the most important in the whole book. The previous chapter on successful RMs is important for those managers looking for pragmatic ways to get ahead in organizations; keys to success, if you will. But for the success of today's *organizations*, for pragmatic ways for them to move ahead in terms of increased productivity and global competitive advantage, the key is the *effectiveness* of their managers. And to reiterate, effective management (as defined by subordinate perceptions of organizational unit performance, both quantity and quality, and subordinate satisfaction and commitment) is most strongly related to communicating and human resource management activities. Obviously, it would be nice if we also had "hard" measures of effectiveness, such as profits, costs, and service. Our type of comprehensive study across diverse organizations wasn't conducive to that sort of measurement, which in any case has to be defined ahead of time; there's no official set of measures, of course. However, we feel confident in our answer to the question: Effective RMs interact with, communicate with, and manage their people more and better than ineffective RMs.

CHAPTER **SIX**
Communication Activities

Manager: *Because I'm on the road so much, I have a scheduled meeting with my people every Monday morning. We rarely have an agenda. It's a discussion meeting to exchange information about our products and to share new methods and procedures that I have picked up on my trips. It's as informal as possible to keep communications open. Everyone participates; no one preaches.*

Subordinate: *He sometimes uses a very formal approach, for example, posting a memo to be initialed by each person in each department. Then he follows it up with a discussion at monthly department meetings. To help him keep abreast of things, he sometimes convenes an on-the-spot meeting with the department heads.*

THE RMS IN THESE SCENARIOS COMMUNICATED WITH their people in a variety of different ways and settings: weekly and monthly meetings, written communication, formal conferences, and casual chats. Our study revealed what connects all these forms of communication: They are some of the most important hallmarks of *effective* management.

As we saw in Figure 3-3, traditional management activities make up a big chunk of RMs' day-to-day activities: about one third of the activities we observed in our study. They are central to management, regardless of their weaker connection to success and effectiveness (as we've defined those goals).

RMs also spend a lot of their time communicating; almost a third of the total amount of RMs' activity we observed in our study was communication of one kind or another. As we have seen, unlike the traditional management activities, communication activities have a strong correlation to one of our goals—effectiveness. While the top third of *successful* RMs did about 10% more of this activity than the bottom third, communication activities impacted RM *effectiveness* far stronger (by 45%) than any other activity. As Figure 6-1 illustrates, RMs spend a lot of their time communicating with subordinates, peers, and superiors; the successful ones, and especially the effective ones, do relatively more.

FIGURE 6-1
Distribution of Communication Activities

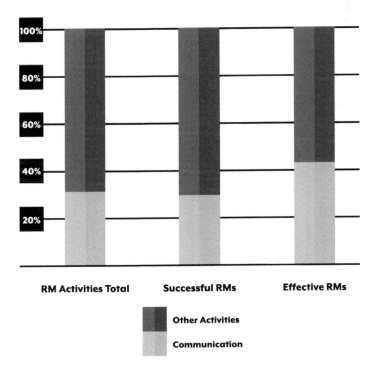

Effective communicators do more than pass information along; they transmit meaning from sender to receiver. That is, effective communication represents more than an order, a request, a set of numbers, or a deadline. It represents both information and its significance: why it matters, where it fits in the bigger picture, who it's important to, and what the end result of transmitting it will be. It's no wonder that management educators and trainers, not to mention Real Managers themselves, see communication as central to management.

We can break the communication process down into five general elements: a sender, the message to be transmitted, the medium used to carry the message, the receiver of the message, and the interpretation given to the message by the receiver. In our study of RMs, we further refined the process into two basic categories of observable behavior:

1. *Exchanging routine information*: this can include answering procedural questions, receiving and disseminating requested information, conveying the results of meetings, giving or receiving routine information over the phone, and holding staff meetings of an informational nature.

2. *Handling paperwork*: some of many examples are organizing email; reading and writing routine reports, memos and letters; doing routine financial reporting and bookkeeping; and carrying out general desk work.

Table 6-1 provides examples from our interviews of how both of these activities were actually carried out by RMs on a day-to-day basis.

TABLE 6-1

*Routine Communication Activities: Some Examples**

EXCHANGING ROUTINE INFORMATION

HIGH AMOUNT	MEDIUM AMOUNT	LOW AMOUNT
Has a formally scheduled meeting with all departmental personnel on a weekly basis to review cost control data and pinpoint problem areas.	Makes it a point to visit with all of the departmental personnel and pass on to them the latest ideas conveyed at monthly managerial meetings.	Posts information sent down from higher management on the employee bulletin board for all to see and read.

HANDLING PAPERWORK

HIGH AMOUNT	MEDIUM AMOUNT	LOW AMOUNT
Makes sure that all cost control reports are completed on time and submitted to the central office.	Reads all incoming correspondence and ensures that any information that should be forwarded to other personnel is done so immediately.	Makes sure that all official memos are reviewed and approved before being sent out.

* These examples are drawn from structured interviews with RMs.

This all might seem commonplace, but these examples belie the importance of communication to successful and effective management, as we began to see in the last chapter. Now we will see how and why this is the case, as we delve into the communication flows in real organizations and examine the major barriers that RMs face in communicating. We also provide some specific guidelines for increasing communication effectiveness. Throughout, we blend judicious doses of management and communication theory with the empirical findings from our study: the experiences of real RMs doing their best to communicate effectively.

COMMUNICATION FLOW

Communication can flow downward, upward, laterally and diagonally in real organizations; RMs use all of these forms to convey and receive routine information. Table 6-2 shows the distribution of these flows as reported by a sample of our RMs. As you might expect, RMs communicate most often to their subordinates in a downward flow, and their subordinates communicate back in an upward flow. The RMs in our study communicated less with their superiors than with their subordinates.

TABLE 6-2
Self-Reported Communication Flows
in Five Diverse Organizations*

TYPES OF COMMUNICATION	DOWNWARD		UPWARD	
	TO SUBORDINATES	FROM SUPERIORS	FROM SUBORDINATES	TO SUPERIORS
Frequency per week (mean)	48.7	13.9	50.6	17.7
Face to Face (percent)	83.4	76.9	81.1	82.4
Phone calls (percent)	10.2	11.4	9.8	12.8
Group meetings (percent)	13.8	19.6	9.0	12.6
Frequency of memos per week (mean)	3.7	3.2	3.4	2.3

* Adapted from Fred Luthans and Janet K. Larsen, "How Managers Really Communicate," Human Relations 39 no. 2 (February 1986): 168. Note that this data was gathered long before the widespread use of email and other forms of electronic communication in the organizational environment.

In addition, RMs reported communicating verbally (face-to-face, over the phone, or in meetings) with both subordinates and superiors more often than they wrote to them. This is one area where today's managers' frequent use of email and texting for writing messages would lead to quite different results from what was observed of the RMs in the earlier study.

Downward Communication

When RMs communicate with their subordinates, they usually have one of two goals in mind: providing instructions and job-related information directly connected with carrying out tasks, and passing along general information related to the organization and unit at large. We call this downward communication. There are many different types of downward channels, including memos, face-to-face conversations, public address systems, bulletin boards, in-house newsletters, and group emails and text alerts. Whatever the method, RMs use downward communication to equip their subordinates with the proper direction, and ultimately as a way to control the outcome of tasks.

However, downward communication doesn't always work well: information gets garbled in the process. For example, verbal information expands as it moves down the line. Simple messages take on additional meanings as they travel from one level to the next. Only a small percentage of all messages that are passed through hierarchical levels emerge in their original form; most have been greatly expanded through reinterpretation. One manager faced the issue this way:

> I know that when information is passed down the line, people like to add their own ideas and interpretations to what is being communicated. I can't stop this. However, during my weekly staff meetings, I put aside a short time at the end to discuss policy changes and other information that has come from the top. I try to get feedback from my staff on what this means to them. If there are any misinterpretations or rumors that need to be handled, I do it then. I can't guarantee that my people are going to always believe what I tell them, but at least I know how they are interpreting all the information that comes down from above.

This RM sought feedback from his staff in a structured setting: a weekly meeting. By getting feedback (upward communication, as we'll see in a bit) this manager did his best to address the problem of reinterpretation.

Another way to deal with garbled communication is to put it in writing; this is especially important when messages must move through more than one level. Information that is considered important should be put in writing if only to have a record of what was really communicated, but most management experts agree that, whenever possible, managers should supplement written communication with oral communication. It's important to get the message out twice. The written statement provides a constant reference that subordinates can consult if clarification is needed; the oral discussion refines points that the RM has not clearly spelled out in the written communication. One manager told us about this communication two-step with his staff:

> Whenever I have a meeting with any of my subordinates and we agree on some new work assignment, I always do

*two things. First, I make sure they know exactly what they
are supposed to be doing. Second, I follow up our meeting
by sending them a memo. In this way, if there has been a
miscommunication, they can get back to me. At the same
time, I have a record of what we agreed on so if there is a
problem later on, I can dig out the memo and review it
with them. I find this approach works really well. My boss
uses it with me and I use it with my people.*

The process of two-step downward communication forms a chain
in the management hierarchy down from the executive level through
RMs and ultimately to their subordinates.

Upward Communication

Upward communication typically flows from subordinate to supe-
rior, providing feedback to managers on how things are going. Using
this upward flow, RMs can gauge how well subordinates understand
the task and their progress in relation to the situation; upward communication also helps create the *esprit de corps* vital to high-quality work.
As Table 6-2 shows, face-to-face conversation was by far the most
common type of upward communication among the managers in our
survey, although email and other forms of electronic communication
would probably give the in-person conversation a run for its money,
especially when employees want to have a formal record of something
that they conveyed to the boss. Upward communication gives subordinates an opportunity to convey their point of view on matters that
are important to them: to drive the conversation, in other words. Conversely, it gives RMs feedback on how well things are going so they can
identify emerging problems before they become serious.

Just like downward flows, upward communication has its problems,
however. Whereas downward verbal communication expands, verbal
information contracts as it goes up the line. This is particularly true
when subordinates communicate bad news. For example, we found
that when a subordinate told an RM something negative or unpleasant (e.g., "Salaries are way too low given the relative amount of work
people in this department do."), the statement was likely couched in
a much milder, briefer message ("Salaries need to be raised.") In other
words, if there is a large amount of verbal information being passed up

the line, bad news tends to be distorted or filtered, while good news arrives almost intact. When RMs get written messages from their subordinates, the ones that get read, remembered, and acted upon are brief, make it easy to implement or make a decision, and lead to clear benefits for the people involved. One manager recognized this in the written communication flowing up from his staff:

> *I insist on getting important information from my subordinates in writing. The everyday things can be verbal. However, either way, I bet that I'm not getting the whole story. My people love to blow good news my way while sweeping bad news under the rug. I've found there's only one way to overcome this habit. I keep my ears open and if I hear some disturbing news through the grapevine, I let my subordinates know about it. I can't run an effective department if people don't tell me everything—good and bad. I think I've been using the grapevine since I took this job, and I believe that all the other effective managers in the company do, too.*

The solution, for this RM? Pay attention to informal communication—"the grapevine"—including lateral communication from other RMs, which is the third kind of communication flow.

Lateral and Diagonal Communication

RMs most often use lateral communication, between managers on the same level of the hierarchy, to promote teamwork and coordination. A similar process, diagonal communication, happens between RMs who are not in the same department or on the same level of the hierarchy; this can be slightly up or slightly down. One manager explained the process:

> *If we're going to get things done around here, we have to know what the right hand and the left hand are doing. Keeping in close touch with the other departments often helps cut through red tape and helps me network throughout the company. It's important to know what's going on around you to keep everyone going in the same direction.*

This manager used lateral and diagonal communication not just to get things done, but also to network—a sure sign of a successful RM.

Indeed, RMs engage in lateral and diagonal communication more often for networking than they do for routine communication (we delve more deeply into networking in Chapter Seven). Still, RMs do sometimes use lateral/diagonal channels to convey general information. But because they draw in people outside the manager's direct sphere of operation and influence, these communication flows can also create problems. One of the most common is that other managers sometimes interpret these cross-communication flows as a power play. For example, "What's Chuck from quality control doing talking to Mary from computer operations? I bet he's trying to get some information about the latest quality control reports before they're made available to the productivity committee." Even if Chuck sees his diagonal communication as simply networking—a route to his personal success—others could interpret it as circumventing established power centers, or even a stab in the back. And they might be right, if the communication harms their own chances for advancement, with or without Chuck's knowledge.

Whether or not such interpretations are true, lateral and diagonal communication can be the basis for rumors that carry erroneous and sometimes harmful information. To minimize the possible problems associated with cross-communication, we formulated some guidelines drawing from the ideas of management experts and supported by the experiences of our effective RMs:

1. *Talk to your boss.* You should consult your immediate boss, if only informally, before formally communicating across departmental lines. In this way, the boss knows what is going on and can shield you from unwarranted criticism.

2. *Keep communicating upward.* You should keep your boss informed of any significant results of the cross-communication. For example, interdepartmental arrangements that call for representatives from each department to coordinate their efforts can lead to better performance for all departments involved. However, if the respective superiors (the bosses of the RMs working on the interdepartmental project) don't know what's going on, they may feel that their subordinates have gone beyond

their authority. Also, any interdepartmental arrangement that benefits one side more than the other is likely to draw the wrath of the boss whose side is being shortchanged. By keeping your bosses in the loop, you can protect yourself from the backlash that is likely to follow an agreement that has unfair advantages.

3. *Follow up in writing.* Unless there is good reason to keep things verbal, you should exchange memos when lateral or diagonal communications result in new work assignments or other job-related changes. This ensures that each party is aware of what is going on. Cross-communication requires care and sensitivity from the effective RM.

DEALING WITH COMMUNICATION BARRIERS

You might have noticed that so far, we've assumed that everyone in any particular communication flow understands what is going on. In other words, we've assumed that the meaning of the communication gets passed perfectly along with the words. But what if this isn't true? Regardless of which type of communication flow is involved, there are always potential barriers that prevent the free and complete transfer of meaning between sender and receiver. How do RMs make sure that their communication is not just heard, but understood? Luckily, we found that many RMs were aware of these barriers and knew useful ways to deal with them. Let's examine these barriers in turn, and how to overcome them.

Perceptual Barriers

Everyone, including RMs, looks at the world through their own rose-colored glasses. Our perception, our own interpretation of reality, depends on our background and life experiences. And just as no two people have ever had exactly the same experiences, no two people perceive things exactly the same way. If empirical reality is the objects, events, and behaviors that people observe, perception is the interpretation of these objects, events, and behaviors that gives them meaning. Meanings can be simple, everyday, and reflexive, and they can also be richly complex and laden with significance. Every RM encounters and processes the meaning of things many times each day, whether they are aware of it or not.

Sometimes, empirical reality and interpretive perception overlap, and empirical reality reinforces the interpretation. For example: you see your boss and another department head loudly exchanging words. The reality? There are two people who are standing close to each other and yelling about something. If you interpret this as two superiors disagreeing over some matter and angrily (and loudly) arguing about it—congratulations, you win! Joking aside, in this example it is likely that your interpretation matches the reality of the situation. Consider another example. A manager receives a memo from the boss that says, effective immediately, all overtime is cancelled and will not be reinstated until the company works down its large backlog of inventory. This is the empirical reality. The RM perceives it to mean that if sales do not pick up in the very near future, the company will start laying people off. Empirical reality, the typed memo, set the stage for interpretive perception, interpreting and expanding the words that were in the memo outside the realm of that message.

Of all the possible causes of communication breakdown, perceptual problems are probably the most common. Management experts, and our RMs on the ground, point to some commonalities about perceptual problems:

1. *Reality is in the eye of the beholder.* People tend to interpret reality to suit themselves. Receivers tend to modify both written and verbal messages mentally to fit their view of reality, or what they would like reality to be.

2. *Know your audience.* To understand the perception a subordinate has of a particular message, a Real Manager has to know that person's background. For example, during hard economic times, union members are likely to interpret cost-saving needs as a prelude to wage concessions or even terminations. When management secures a new, large, government contract and announces that it will start hiring in the near future, many current employees who might otherwise see the new contract as a chance for overtime will instead interpret this announcement to mean that management will only hire to fill the production gap not addressed through overtime work.

3. *Perception means rationalization.* Perception tends to be defensive and protective. People performing below expectations are

more likely to see their poor performance as a result of external conditions (for example, lack of effort from supporting personnel, poor equipment, or inadequate training provided by the company) rather than of internal conditions (like poor personal work habits, lack of skill, or low motivation). When management decrees performance-related job cuts—"getting rid of dead wood"—many employees think other people's jobs are at stake instead of their own, thanks to defensive perception.

4. *Perception plays a particularly important role in verbal communications.* People tend to remember those parts of a verbal message that agree with their own position and downplay or forget those parts that conflict with it. In other words, listeners alter or change the overall message to suit their point of view. For example, one RM told us about a situation involving pay raises:

> *A few months ago, I convinced my boss that we should allocate at least some money for merit and not have our usual across-the-board raises. However, I made a big mistake. I told my best worker what was about to happen and that he could look forward to a hefty raise. Unfortunately, by the time he told everyone else, the story was completely changed. According to the latest rumor I've heard, there are to be no more automatic raises—only merit raises. That's not what I told him! I did manage to save the day, however, by putting out a memo that spelled out exactly how raises would be handled in the future. Now all I have to do is hope my boss doesn't find out that I'm the one who leaked the initial story to a talkative subordinate.*

The difference between verbal and written communication in this example is stark. Like a game of telephone, office chatter made the original message unrecognizable; the situation was only saved when the RM put it in writing. This is not to say that written communication beats verbal in every situation, just that RMs should be aware of the pitfalls and advantages of each.

5. *Written communication reduces message distortion.* Because there are fewer opportunities to translate or freely interpret the message, the original intent of the message—not to mention its actual text—comes through better in writing. A well-written communication typically results in far less distortion than a well-spoken message.

Inference Barriers

People read between the lines, in writing and in conversation. In doing so, they make inferences—assumptions not in the original message. Just as empirical reality and perception can overlap, so can inference and perception. When a message is unclear or ambiguous, receivers will draw inferences that are in line with their own way of thinking. This can be a problem. Particularly in written communication, unclear messaging demands assumptions to fill in perceived gaps in the text. And the greater the number of inferences required, the more likely it is that the sender's intended meaning will not be the same as the receiver's interpreted meaning. Effective RMs can nip inference problems in the bud by following these guidelines:

1. *Clear, concise, self-explanatory written communication.* Written messages need to be as crystal clear as possible. To ensure that they are, the sender should build in some time between the writing of the message and its conveyance. This gives the sender time to reread and edit the material with a relatively fresh eye.

2. *Outside editing.* When possible, the sender should have important written communication checked by a trusted associate to ensure that the directive or policy is clear to them. If it is not, rewrite.

3. *Feedback process.* In verbal communication, there should be time for feedback from receivers (for example, a staff meeting to answer questions or address concerns). This feedback allows the manager to explain the message and deal with objections or problems, including misperceptions that, if not handled now, will crop up later. The RM can learn much from nonverbal cues (especially facial expressions) in this context. One RM made the importance of answering questions and providing feedback particularly clear:

We had a memo come down from the top brass a few months ago. It related to the new layoff policy and whoever wrote it must have copied it directly out of the union-management contract without adding any explanation. The essence of the memo was that in case of a layoff, those who were hired last would be dropped first. However, there was nothing about the fact that those with seniority in other departments could return to their old units and bump people there who had less seniority than they did. The memo wasn't incorrect, but it was incomplete. We almost had a riot on our hands. Whoever wrote the memo should have clarified the fact that the message related only to intradepartmental policy regarding layoffs. Better yet, he should have added a section on bumping. In any event, it was necessary for the top management and the top union officials to follow up with another memo to explain the rights of those who were laid off in a particular department. What you don't tell people seems to cause as many problems as what you do tell them.

"What you don't tell people"—this RM described a classic inference barrier. In this case, the misperception was corrected with further, and more clearly written communication.

Language Barriers

The structure and meaning of a series of words in a message is a language. Language barriers afflict much more than communication between people from different countries. Language can become a barrier to communication any time the receiver is unfamiliar with a particular arrangement of words or misinterprets their meaning. Miscommunication between people from different cultures is a familiar story. Consider, for example, a new salesperson required to attend bimonthly staff meetings at the home office. She proceeds to take half a day to come to the office two weeks later, only to find that the meetings are every two months and not twice a month.

Language barriers, even ones caused by people simply defining words differently, can cause significant problems. For example, many organizations use the word "burn" for "photocopy." Unless new employees are made familiar with the jargon of the trade, the individual who is told to "burn this original set of blueprints" is likely to destroy the materials. In other words, because the receiver of the message wasn't even aware that there is a language problem (that there is a different definition of "burn") he didn't take corrective action until it was too late and the fatal mistake had been made. And the problem is not restricted to the organization itself: new suppliers, customers, clients, and others who come into contact with it are likely to be subjected to this trade jargon and just as likely to respond incorrectly.

How should RMs work towards overcoming language barriers and achieving smooth, clear communication? Here's what our study suggests:

1. *Words matter—a lot.* As part of the socialization process, all new organization members, as well as key outsiders, should be made aware of specialized jargon. This is particularly important when a word or phrase has a totally different meaning than it does in general practice. One RM we talked to made language a key part of new employees' introduction to the company:

    > *In my department, I make it a point to talk to all of my new people the first day they're on the job. Then I schedule another meeting with them during their third or fourth week. During this session, I try to find out how well they have learned the ropes, the jargon, the informal rules, and everything else they ought to know. It's all right to be naive when you first come in here, but I expect this to be overcome within a couple of weeks. If it isn't, I want to know why. Sometimes there are things that the new hire still hasn't been told or hasn't learned. In other cases, he is just too slow and has to be told again. In any case, I want this problem solved—and fast. It's the only way to bring new people up to speed and prevent a disaster around here.*

This RM recognized the importance of jargon and unwritten rules in socializing new employees, and pursued clear communication with multiple in-person meetings.

2. *Bring outsiders up to speed.* Managers should encourage all new employees, as well as key outside figures, to ask questions related to operations and procedures. If the RM doesn't have the time or knowledge to answer all of their questions, she should assign an experienced subordinate, or whoever the appropriate knowledgeable employee is, to answer the newcomer or outsider's questions.

3. *Meanings change as people change.* Keep in mind that meanings are not in words, they are in people. The way people interpret a word dictates what that word means to them. For example, telling a subordinate to "get this report completed as soon as possible" may result in the person dropping whatever he's doing and focusing exclusively on the report. Another subordinate might interpret this same message to mean that when she has finished with the financial data analysis she's running, she should move on to the new report. Adding a clarifying statement can avoid such problems.

Status Barriers

People in any group, organization or society habitually rank their compatriots relative to each other: this is what we call status. Status is extremely important, especially in organizational settings, because it lends credibility to those in higher-level positions. CEOs tend to be more believable because of their position than department heads; they have greater status. Similarly, at least in the eyes of top management, a supervisor is more credible than a worker. Status problems in organizations happen when people give greater weight to *who* people are, rather than *what* they are saying (and the evidence, or lack thereof, that backs up that point of view). Judgments about status are hard to avoid, but nobody's status should trump their message, its content, and its viability.

There are a couple of important things to know about status as a communication barrier, as we learned from the RMs in our study:

1. *The communicator's status influences the message's credibility.* This can result in blind acceptance or rejection of messages. In

order to discourage these kinds of snap judgments, it's important for RMs to foster honest, open feedback. As an RM, you can minimize status problems by letting your subordinates know that you want to be given accurate information, and reward those who provide it.

2. *Knowledge and experience makes communication more accurate.* When RMs have these two qualifications, their formal status becomes a minor issue. Their subordinates often regard RMs who "have the facts" as more credible than higher status managers who lack such knowledge.

RMs can deal with status barriers by trying hard to be straightforward and unpretentious, letting their knowledge take center stage. One RM applied this principle to meetings:

> *When I hold small meetings in my office, I make it a point to de-emphasize my position in the company. I don't think you can be effective unless everyone feels equal. I try to create this type of environment by gathering everyone around a large round table that I have in my office. I get out from behind my desk and sit with my people. Now, this doesn't guarantee that status won't be a problem, but I think it is a way of minimizing it.*

This RM recognized that physical space is part of status; even staying behind the desk in one's office can create a status barrier. He dealt with it by rearranging the physical space to avoid the potential status barrier and make it possible to communicate clearly and directly with his team.

EFFECTIVE COMMUNICATION ACTIVITIES OF RMS

We used a simple definition of "communication activity" in our study. It consisted of two observable, everyday things: exchanging routine information and processing paperwork. On the surface, these aren't as exotic or sophisticated as the terms and communication functions that the traditional managerial communication literature talks about. Instead, they are real-world equivalents of those theoretical functions; they encompass the same processes and dimensions that the scholarly analyses do. Let's review some of these deeper processes. Our goal is to reach a better understanding of how RMs communicate, what they do to improve the effectiveness of communication, and how those everyday communication activities, when done well, represent effective communication.

There are four steps to effective communication: attention, understanding, acceptance, and action. Together, these steps create communication that is most likely to clearly convey information and message. Leave one out and what happens? Management theorists suggest, and our study confirms, that communication will break down.

Attention

The first step for the effective RM is to snap their audience's focus right to the message they want to send. Attention happens when the message sender—the RM—convinces the receiver to concentrate on the message and to screen out all disturbances and distractions. This means overcoming message competition. Here's how:

1. *Start with a bang.* Use something striking or singular, like a visual, a set of figures, or a fact, as an immediate attention-getter. For example, one of the RMs told us that when he gave a presentation to the finance committee asking for more funding, he would always present what the main competitor was doing in this area of the business. Because the competitor's funds were usually greater, he could always get the committee's attention.

2. *Know what the audience wants.* Focus on something that is of primary importance to the receiver. If the receiver is interested in trimming expenses, gear your communication to cost-cutting steps. If your audience is concerned with productivity, explain how the plan will lower the cost per unit of production.

Understanding

Why is it that many RMs realize the importance of achieving understanding, but time and again fail to achieve it? Understanding requires comprehension on the part of the receiver, but more fundamentally, requires a straightforward and fair relationship between manager and subordinate. Understanding is a two-way street.

Too often, if an RM thinks the receiver does not comprehend their message, they ask, "Do you understand what I've just said (or written) to you?" The receiver of the message almost always says, "Yes." The problem is that the pressure is on the receiver to say yes no matter what, particularly in the case of downward communication (when they are receiving communication from their boss). Few people are going to admit to their boss, "I lost you about five seconds into what you were saying."

Instead of asking receivers if they understand, RMs should ask *what* they understand. This gives receivers a chance to put the message into their own words; and if they are incorrect the sender can say, "No, that's not what I meant to convey. Here's what I'm trying to say." Effective communication often means patiently restating the message again and again. Don't ask *if*, ask *what*.

Acceptance

The third step in effective communication, acceptance, happens when the receiver is willing to go along with the message. Quite often this compliance is automatic; the RM asks a subordinate to do something and the individual does it, because it's the boss's orders. This sort of unquestioning acceptance (which, of course, may very well be grudging, which brings its own set of problems) is common in strongly hierarchical organizations. But acceptance can get short-circuited when RMs don't communicate effectively. Of course, successful acceptance depends from the start on the first two steps of communication going well: getting the receiver's attention and ensuring that they understand the message. But the receiver can put up a roadblock to the message even if they understand it perfectly well.

What happens when the receiver of a message understands it, but rejects it out of hand? That puts an end to effective communication, especially if the sender doesn't recognize that their message just got rejected. For example, when Japanese industry began to challenge perceived American dominance in the 1980s, the struggles of American managers to communicate effectively with their Japanese counterparts received much attention (a struggle that continues to this day). Japanese managers avoid simply saying no; such outright and obvious rejections are to be avoided in Japanese culture. What seems like equivocation (avoiding the question, putting it off to a later time, or offering what sounds like a maybe) to the Western manager is often actually the Japanese manager's way of saying no. In this case, the pressure is on the American manager to both recognize the rejection, and to recast the message in order to gain acceptance.

This communication barrier is not limited to cultural difference; it happens in many situations during which the receiver resists a message and the sender doesn't pick up on or understand their resistance. For example, a subordinate may already be overburdened with work and unable to drop everything to find a particular report that has been mislaid. Or the subordinate may feel that they lack the proper training to carry out the task. For example, the subordinate might say, "I don't know anything about printing files using that program. But if it can wait until after lunch, Bob will be back and he can take care of it." However, if the RM pushes and says, "There's nothing to it. Get in there and try it, you'll get the hang of it almost immediately," the manager is refusing to acknowledge the subordinate's lack of acceptance. Sometimes this is a good idea, because it forces people to train themselves in jobs that they might not voluntarily undertake; other times, the RM is making a mistake by pushing the matter. One manager in our study made this distinction clear:

> I generally have people respond very quickly to me, but I may not get the results I want. When I tell them something, I emphasize two things: what needs to be done and what type of assistance or support will be provided. Look, if I ask someone to fill out the monthly cost control report and he's never done it before, he's not going to be very receptive to my comments about this being good training. In fact, he thinks he's being dumped on. What I try to do is provide him with previous reports, call in someone who has done these reports before and have this expert brief him on what to do. Then I make myself available to answer questions or get additional assistance if he needs it. People don't mind going the extra mile for you if they think you'll be there for them if they run into trouble.

This RM was willing to push his staff to learn new skills, but recognized the importance of effective communication to make sure those tasks actually got done.

Apart from the importance of understanding message resistance, our study emphasized two crucial keys to gain acceptance:

1. *Feedback* (both verbal and nonverbal) from the receiver is important. If you give an order or directive and don't allow your subordinate to say anything about it, you can only infer acceptance—you don't really know. If your subordinate has a problem with the directive, their rejection won't show up until their work is either late or incorrectly done. You should not only tolerate feedback, you should encourage it.

2. *Persistence.* If the task is important enough, the effective RM doesn't take no for an answer. As an effective RM, you should get subordinates the training or assistance they need to get the job done, and give them moral support and the necessary coaching along the way. However, you also must get subordinates to accept the order by using effective persuasion. Your words and actions are both key in this process. Finally, the effective RM relies on threats or disciplinary punishment only when all else fails.

The Importance of Simple, Repetitive Language

The simpler a message, the more likely it will be understood and acted upon properly. Simplicity takes two forms: direct and complete. Direct simplicity means that the message gets to the point without providing information that is supplementary, tangential, or simply filler. Complete simplicity means that when the message has been relayed, the listener understands everything that the communicator wanted understood.

Simple messages should not be so brief that they leave out salient facts. When the message contains a series of important facts, complex analyses, or difficult-to-digest quantitative data, repetitiveness helps. By repeating or restating these important facts, the sender increases the likelihood of complete comprehension. The RM should take care with repetitiveness, but it can be harnessed in at least three ways:

1. *Simple words are more powerful than sophisticated words.* Although there is always the possibility of talking down to listeners, it is far more common for RMs to confuse them by using words that they do not understand than by using words that are below their level of understanding. Always strive for simplicity and clarity in your message.

2. *Repeat the major points, then recap.* Repeating yourself may feel trite or unnecessary. It is not. In fact, most listeners welcome repetition of important ideas because it helps them keep track of what is being said. Effective RMs know that every message should be understood. If the subject matter is complex, you should communicate it in manageable portions, giving listeners the opportunity to ask questions or seek clarification. Additionally, if you recap the message as they go along, listeners will find it much easier to follow the flow of information.

3. *Do not belabor the point.* Determine what is to be said and say it. If the communication contains bad news, an effective RM can prepare the other person for it with introductory remarks that explain the reason for the news. For example, if there is to be a layoff and the individual is to be one of those to be let go, you can start by saying that economic conditions have made the action necessary and that some good people will have to be laid off. Then, after telling the individual that he or she is included in this group, you can go over the types of assistance the firm provides or the letter of recommendation that the individual can expect. The remarks should be kept brief and the other person given a chance to talk; if nothing else, the individual will probably want to let off steam.

The Importance of Empathizing

When you empathize, you put yourself in another person's place. Through empathy, effective RMs see things the way their superiors and subordinates do, and can begin to know when to concentrate on work and when to focus on people. Empathy makes it possible to answer questions like "What type of direction does this subordinate need? When should I follow up, and when should I get out of the way?"

Empathy is of particular importance at two stages of the communication process: acceptance and action. When a manager gives an order that a subordinate is reluctant to accept, the effective RM notices the subordinate's hesitancy through such nonverbal cues as facial expressions. For whatever reason, the subordinate may not understand how important the matter is or how significant her role will be. Empathy helps the RM determine the best way to communicate this importance and jump-starts the action stage. The empathetic RM stays alert for signs that the subordinate needs assistance (and makes sure this assistance actually gets provided). One RM in our study described the importance of this kind of careful, active empathy:

> *I try to get to know my people so I know what's important to them. When I have to assign work, I know when to be flexible and when to push hard… Last month, the wife of one of our employees had a baby. The fellow was scheduled to go on a trip to the West Coast the following week. He called from the hospital, gave me the news, and asked if he could postpone the trip. It wasn't necessary—when I checked the assignment calendar earlier, I knew that his wife would be having the baby at about the same time he was scheduled to be out of town, so I had a replacement ready to move in. All it took was a little forward planning. Once I know what's important to my people in terms of their career development and personal life, I try to adjust the job to reflect this. The result is usually a win-win situation for my people, me, and—I know this sounds hokey—for the company.*

Hokey? Perhaps—just like repeating yourself and recapping. To your subordinates, however, it's just good management.

There are two points you should keep in mind about empathy:

1. *Empathy is a result of understanding people's needs.* It can be improved by allowing subordinates the opportunity to communicate upward and by interacting with them continually. In this way, effective RMs begin to obtain deeper insight into how their people feel about issues and what can be done to manage them more effectively. This point really drives home the importance

of in-person communication and follow-up; it not only leads to action, it continually improves the communication process itself by fueling empathy. This is a process that builds upon itself over time.

2. *Be empathetic; don't be a pushover.* Effective RMs don't lose sight of the fact that their task is to improve performance and get the job at hand accomplished. Empathy can help, but it does not mean that the RM should acquiesce to her employees' every need and desire. Effective RMs know that they sometimes have to ask their people to do things that are difficult or unpleasant. Your first responsibility is to get things done, not to keep subordinates happy. However, also remember that happy subordinates get things done, and that your subordinates don't always know what will lead them to a fulfilling work life. A difficult, unpleasant task could potentially be a life-changer.

The Importance of Understanding Body Language

Body language is one of the most important forms of nonverbal communication. Although silent, it is a language like any other, and takes many different forms: everything from posture, to eye movement and eye contact, to facial and hand movements. Even where a person stands in a room in relation to others can be an important signal. Although everybody uses body language, many are unaware that they do. Here are some tips for RMs to effectively interpret body language:

1. *Eye contact is important but equivocal.* Looking people directly in the eye is often, but not always, a sign of honesty. Good liars are able to look people right in the eye with no compunction; they have come to realize that eye contact is important to convincing their audience. However, you can get some idea of how much stress someone is enduring by looking them in the eye. For example, when right-handed people are trying to deal with an issue on an emotional level, they tend to look to their left. The reverse is true for left-handed people.

2. *That dead-fish handshake really is telling.* Touch is an important way of conveying confidence, trust, or friendship. A firm handshake is regarded as a sign of self-assurance, while a limp

grip signals diffidence, lack of confidence, or even fear. RMs also use touch to convey power relationships. For example, a manager who wants to emphasize an order may grasp the subordinate's arm while issuing the order. However, you have to be careful not to appear to be harassing or bullying. A touch on the shoulder can be a sign of positive attention, but it can also be uncomfortable, or a perceived prelude to something even worse. It all depends on the power relationship between you and your subordinate (and between you and your boss). If you've spent time cultivating empathy with your subordinates, determining that relationship will be much easier. In the end, touching can reinforce your message but must be sensibly and selectively used according to individual and cultural norms.

3. *Physical location can help convey messages.* Where you sit or stand in a room in relation to your subordinates may dictate the style and tenor of the message. When giving commands, you can convey greater authority if you stand up while your subordinate remains seated; you're looking down at your subordinate as you deliver (for example) a reprimand. You can establish authority in the office through something as simple as the furniture layout. For example, by placing the desk as far away from the entrance as possible, you increase your perceived authority, because distance typically is equated with power. This spatial calculus has multiple dimensions. You might try, for example, keeping all visitors on the other side of the desk, using the desk as a wall between you and your visitors, or placing the desk directly in front of a window so that visitors look into the sunlight while you have the sun behind your back. On the other hand, if you want to convey a friendly image, come out from behind the desk and sit on the opposite side with visitors. This eliminates the desk as a barrier and quickly establishes a warm, open environment.

4. *Dress for success.* Even clothing can be used to convey messages. Literature on the topic suggests that the most authoritative pattern for men is the dark pinstripe suit, followed by the solid, the chalk stripe, and the plaid. For women in business, a conservative, tailored suit carries more authority than

a more fashionable suit. Paying attention to seemingly minor details like dress and grooming gives your communication an extra edge.

The Importance of Feedback

Giving and getting feedback is perhaps the primary way effective RMs communicate. Effective feedback can overcome any communication barrier, and the number of methods you can use to give or solicit feedback is legion. The simplest is to directly ask your subordinates for feedback. Try one of these phrases:

- "Can you tell me more about . . .?"
- "You've given me some things to think about. I'd welcome any additional ideas you might have along these lines."
- "I think that we're ready to begin implementation of this project. What do you think?"

Each of these questions encourages subordinates to expand on their earlier comments or to voice an opinion regarding what to do now. They advance the communication and prompt your colleague to demonstrate their own expertise. Asking for feedback will also get you into the mode of listening. It is both a motivating challenge and a constructive compliment to your employee.

Asking for feedback and, more important, really listening to the response is essential to getting subordinates involved in the communication process and, ultimately, decision-making. Effective RMs know that useful feedback depends on making the other party feel free to comment at the outset, and then signaling that they've come through with valuable input. Understand, even if your subordinate is wrong or off-base in some way, their input is in fact valuable because it advances the communication process and gives you both a chance to collaborate on a solution. It's rarely a good idea to shut down an employee who gets off-track in their feedback; instead, work to bring them back into focus by valuing their input. One of the best ways to ensure this is to keep the tone of your conversation positive, as one manager attested:

When I'm trying to give or get feedback, I follow one simple rule: make the other guy look good. I emphasize the positive rather than the negative. I never say, "How come things in your unit are all screwed up?" That's not going to get me anywhere. Instead, I review the positive aspects up to this point and ask how I can help the person get back on track if things are not going too well. I approach these matters by making it clear that we're all in this together. You'd be surprised how much people will open up when they find that your objective is to help them rather than catch them doing something wrong.

It's important to note that this RM's positive tone and willingness to listen is not a pose or a trick. It is instead a true learning posture: a willingness to listen to feedback and act on it.

If step one is getting your subordinates talking by encouraging feedback, step two is sustaining the flow of information—keeping them talking. Encourage this kind of continuing communication by using phrases or statements that sustain the action, like:

- "I understand what you're saying, but tell me, what else do you think we need to do?"
- "Right, right. This all makes a lot of sense. Keep going."
- "What else?"
- "I appreciate what you're saying. It's right in line with the way we've been thinking about approaching this problem. However, how would you handle the implementation phase of this idea? Whom would you include? How long would it take to get this all carried out? Give me more details on the specifics of your approach."

Sustaining the flow of information gets you on the road to real results; it's a way to dig in to the nuts and bolts of the problem at hand. It also builds the confidence of your people over the long term. That's *Real Management*: solving the immediate problem at the same time you're creating a stronger team for future situations.

Finally, don't worry if you think you're repeating yourself. It can be vitally important to provide additional information that elaborates or clarifies what has already been said. Fearing overkill, some RMs are reluctant to do this because they think that their people already understand the message. In other cases, RMs may assume that if their subordinates wanted more information they would ask for it. Actually, many subordinates are reluctant to solicit information from their boss for fear of appearing unsure of themselves or, even worse, unqualified. Silence—and poor communication—is the result.

To sidestep this reluctance to ask questions, you can provide feedback without being asked to do so. Effective RMs in our study prefaced their feedback with an introductory question that allowed subordinates to say, "No, I already understand that. It's not necessary to go on." They also tended to use an introductory remark that was congratulatory in tone, while giving feedback at the same time. For example:

- "I read your report and think that it covers all of the important areas that need to be addressed. However, I'd like to share with you a couple of ideas for expanding it and incorporating more of the cost-related data."
- "I read your report very closely. I like it. What sets it apart from the others I've gone through is . . ."
- "Your progress on this subject has brought you to the point where we need to determine your next step. I'd like to give you my ideas on how we should proceed."

In each of these scenarios, the RM approaches the feedback from the standpoint of the receiver. Each comment conveys something of help or value, and furthermore encourages the receiver to listen to what is coming next.

The Importance of Speaking and Writing Skills

We hear more and more that managers, especially younger managers just out of college, don't speak or write well. In an age of brief, instant communication sent by email, text, and tweet without much thought or preparation, this problem has only become more glaring. As managers move up the hierarchy, basic communication skills become more and more important, and deficiencies in vocal expression and written style, syntax, and even grammar become more glaring (especially since the audience keeps getting larger and larger). We're not suggesting every RM needs to go back to grammar school, but here are some strategies to punch up and clarify your forms of communication:

1. *Know your audience.* Before speaking or writing to anyone, effective RMs have an idea of what their audience is interested in hearing or learning about, and gear their message to the audience's interests. Knowing your audience includes thinking about how broad it is; are you speaking to the entire company, or one small work group? Adjust your speech accordingly.

2. *Have an attention-getting opener.* Make the audience want to learn more. In written communication, start with a fact or statistic that the reader may be unaware of and use this to lead into the rest of the message. In a formal talk, decide whether a short story or joke is in order. (For example, an after-dinner talk should have one; an in-house presentation to senior-level managers should not.) Then briefly relate what the talk is going to be about, and begin.

3. *Get feedback before you go public.* If you're giving a talk, have a colleague listen and offer suggestions on style and content. Have a trusted colleague read over and critique your written communication. RMs use this feedback to improve their overall communication style. In addition, don't automatically dismiss what might seem to be nitpicking; clear, elegant grammar and syntax can make written communication much more impactful.

4. *Close with a bang.* Just as it is important to start off with a bang to get attention, it is also important to have a memorable story or point for summarizing the key points of a talk. This often makes for a powerful closing paragraph or page for a long memo or report.

Listening

Of all the ways managers communicate, listening is one of the most important—but it's probably the most overlooked. It's hard to overstate the importance of developing effective listening skills. Simply put, effective Real Managers know how to listen. Here are some tips:

1. *Message over delivery.* Listen to *what* your employees say rather than *how* they say it. Instead of dismissing the speaker as boring or uninteresting, the effective RM lets the person speak and focuses on the message. When listening, be careful about evaluating body language; as we outlined earlier, it can

be misinterpreted. Pay close attention to the *what* before you jump to the hidden *how* (see #6 below).

2. *Don't interrupt.* Give speakers a chance to convey their message. Hear them out. You should always assume that the other person has something important to say; in this way, you focus your attention more closely on the *what* that they are trying to communicate.

3. *Practice active listening.* Encourage speakers to stay on the main topic by asking them pertinent questions that redirect them back to it. You should also fight the tendency to tune the speaker out when the presentation becomes overly technical or too difficult to understand. Focus on listening, learning, and remembering. Integrate everything the speaker is saying so that it all fits into a logical composite. If any information does not fit into this overall scheme, put it aside and try to integrate it later or have the speaker clarify.

4. *Imitation is flattery.* Try to learn how to improve your own communication by picking up tips from listening to others. For example, in a formal presentation, did the person effectively use audiovisual equipment? Were they able to work in a lot of facts while keeping the presentation lively and interesting, or did they use an emotional appeal that persuaded people to accept their point of view?

5. *Just the facts.* Evaluate the relevance of what you're listening to. Does it include new or useful data that can be of personal value?

6. *Hear what isn't said.* Listen first to what people are expressing out loud to you, but while you're doing that, try as much as possible to pay close attention to intended meanings—things unsaid that the speaker nevertheless intends to communicate. Here's where the care you take in studying body language can pay off in spades. Is the speaker trying to convey any hidden messages? What are they? How do they influence the overall content of the message?

7. *Be a responsive listener.* Maintain eye contact with speakers and give them positive feedback, such as nods of agreement and bright facial expressions. Pay attention to your own body language!

8. *Accept the challenge of effective listening.* Effective RMs recognize that strong, clear communication depends as much on listening as talking. In most cases, they have taught themselves to do it well; it's not something you're born with, nor is it taught in business schools.

A FINAL WORD

No Real Manager exists in a vacuum; routine communication is the air RMs breathe in their day-to-day work lives. As we saw in earlier chapters, communication most directly applies to managerial effectiveness. In fact, of the four major activities of RMs we observed—networking, traditional management functions, human resource management, and routine communication—the communication activity relatively played the most significant role for *effective* managers. These effective RMs communicate in the ways we have described in this chapter, and there is a great deal we can learn from them.

Notice that we haven't said much about success. If, as we have argued, success and effectiveness are two different things, what about the activities that lead to success—to moving up the ladder? We will discuss those activities next.

CHAPTER **SEVEN**

Networking Activities: The Empirical Backdrop

Subordinate: He is always on the telephone, keeping contacts with other managers, with customers, and with suppliers. When he isn't on the job at the firm, he's out developing contacts in the community or attending some meeting.

Colleague: She is always out getting volunteer workers or volunteer speakers. I used to worry about her becoming too involved in community affairs, but she seems to be able to select those people who are likely to support us.

O UT OF ALL THE MANAGEMENT ACTIVITIES WE STUDIED, the difference between successful and effective Real Managers was most obvious in how much, and how well, they networked. That is, by any technique of analysis we used, networking had the closest relationship to success of any management activity, but had the weakest relationship to effectiveness. This was perhaps the single most consistent and interesting finding in our entire study of RMs, and is also surely among the most striking and important. Real Managers network about as frequently as they engage in the other major activities we studied, but *successful* RMs network far more than their peers (see Figure 7-1). For these striving RMs, networking is definitely related to getting ahead and being successful, but it is not related to being effective.

FIGURE 7-1
Distribution of Networking Activities

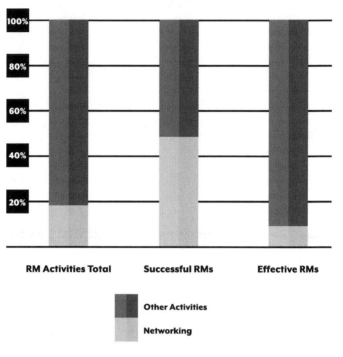

What exactly is networking? Any manager will have an intuitive sense of this activity, but we needed to be more precise. We defined the *networking activity* as a combination of the observable behavioral categories of *socializing/politicking* (non-work-related chit chat, informal joking around, discussing rumors, complaining, griping, downgrading others, and gamesmanship) and *interacting with outsiders* (engaging with people such as customers, suppliers, and vendors in contexts including public relations, external meetings, and community service). A more conceptual, comprehensive definition would state that networking is a system of interconnected or cooperating individuals, and is closely associated with the dynamics of power and the use of social and political skills. Regardless of how we define it, networking, as RMs know, is really about "pressing the flesh," or as one manager explained:

> *I have found that the best way to get ahead around here is to be friendly with people. Treat them as individuals.*

Get to know them, what their backgrounds and inter-
ests are. Kid around with them. Then when you need
them, they will be there for you, whether it is helping
you meet a deadline or giving positive feedback about
you when appraisals or promotion time rolls around. I
have found that this works with my boss as well as with
my subordinates.

This gets to the heart of why (and how) RMs network. They use social and political skills to get ahead in their organizations. In this case, the RM deliberately recognized and employed networking as a managerial strategy for career success. We should emphasize that we don't mean "pressing the flesh" in a disingenuous way (although perhaps it can sometimes be that). The RM above likely genuinely enjoyed getting to know her colleagues as individuals, and her genuine concern and sense of fun shone through. People can usually spot the proverbial used car salesman a mile away.

Many successful RMs use networking without employing it so consciously. But whether a deliberate strategy or not, the results of our study are very clear: the most successful RMs exhibit relatively more networking activity (more by far than any other single activity) than do less successful ones. Equally important, effective RMs (as defined by subordinate satisfaction, commitment, and organizational effectiveness) do relatively the least amount of this activity.

This chapter explores the various facets of this important, but traditionally overlooked, managerial activity. First, we consider networking in terms of interpersonal capabilities: informal organizational networks, power dynamics, and social/political skills. These are the one-on-one and group dynamics that, put together, create the networks. Second, we look at the more formal dimensions and analyses of networking: mentoring, the usefulness of networks, and the impact of networks.

THE INFORMAL ORGANIZATION BECOMES THE REAL ORGANIZATION

Org charts and organizational policies are supposed to clearly delineate all lines of authority and communication. Certainly, this is implied in traditional management literature. It may also be true of the *formal* organization (the organization as officially represented by the

chart and policies), based on its officially prescribed goals and relationships. These include official policies representing areas such as
equal employee opportunity; advancement of employees on the basis
of merit; service to the consumer, client, or patient; product or service
quality; and the public good. This formality can extend to the chain
of command and communication protocols (who may communicate
with whom, and what, how, and when they should communicate),
which are usually—in the formal sense—a matter of written record in
the form of company policies and procedures or the organization chart.

RMs may feel free to scoff at the preceding paragraph. As they all
know, organizational structure goes much deeper than the carefully
delineated procedures and relationships defined in the organization's
formal structure. Within every formal organization are one or more
informal organizations (shadow organizations, if you will) with unofficial goals, norms, and relationships; groups of employees who share
common beliefs and goals that transcend (or perhaps subvert) formal
organization goals. Informal organizations can have economic, security,
or social purposes, and can be found at the operating level of an organization or in supervisory, staff, or executive circles. A group of production
workers who restrict line work or a "good old boy" network of higher-
level managers are examples of informal organizations: they have relationships quite different than those defined by the formal organization.

When in conflict with the formal organization, the informal organization might have different, even competing objectives; it can restrict
output, block a group or individual's ambition, or resist change of all
kinds. Anyone who's ever grumbled about their boss with their coworkers intuitively understands this sort of subversive purpose.

The more interesting case is when the informal organization benefits the formal one. This can happen in myriad ways. Informal organizations can:

- Act as a backup for the formal organization, providing
  substantive resources to accomplish formal goals.
- Supplement formal communication channels with useful,
  practical, unofficial ones, especially upward and horizontal.
  (Think perhaps of an informal network of executive assistants,
  who talk amongst themselves and provide a back-channel to
  the big boss.)

- Provide a flexible framework that complements the real-life strengths and weaknesses of the organization's employees at all levels.
- Reduce the overload on individual employees or groups.
- Motivate employees to reach formally designated goals. (Like a manager who buys dinner for his group if they meet a sales goal.)
- Satisfy a variety of individual and group needs.

In real organizations, informal organizations are inevitable and often very powerful. As new employees are socialized into the organization, they quickly learn that to survive and succeed they must join one or more informal organizations. In fact, from the RM's perspective, the "real" organization is a composite of the formal and informal organizations, and he or she must master and use both of them.

Here are some of the key points to recognize about informal organizations:

- They exist at all levels in every organization.
- They are inevitable.
- They can be beneficial, detrimental, or both, depending on the situation.
- They can be very powerful, even more powerful than the formal organization.
- The "real" organization includes the formal and one or more informal organizations.

POWER: THE NAME OF THE GAME

The importance of informal organizations as supplements or checks to the formal hierarchy highlights the dimension of power in networking. No RM can succeed or even survive in modern organizations without power, whether it is the possession of formal authority, deliberate control over others in informal networks, or simply a degree of influence. Power can be viewed as a commodity, a medium, or an object of exchange, and it plays a complex and central role in day-to-day management—especially in its relationship to managerial success.

For successful RMs, power is a commodity; it's the accumulated raw material that can be bought, sold, or forged into the things that allow them to move up in the hierarchy. When we think of power this way, it is easier to see how it applies to specific situations. For example: power can be the ability to affect a specific budget line item, the authority to get specific resources to meet a production or report deadline, or the capacity to make an impressive quick showing (to demonstrate almost immediate results). One manager said:

> *I have always had the knack of being able to marshal the necessary resources when I really need them, to get the job done. It may be that I ask for a favor from someone or that I demand something from someone else. But if I need something, I can usually get it.*

This RM didn't even need to know where his power came from. To him it was instinctive—a "knack." It is likely, however, that he accumulated it from networking in informal organizations.

Popular management literature usually oversimplifies the discussion of power. We wanted to provide a more fine-grained definition, so we classified power in several ways: the sources of power, the situations in which it is used, and the value systems of the people who are influenced by power (targets of influence).

To begin with, power, unlike love, does not grow with sharing. It cannot be simultaneously shared, because inevitably one sharer can, or must, preempt the power of another. Therefore, distributing or seizing power is sometimes a zero-sum-game: if one person gains power, the other loses. However, not all power relationships are win-lose situations: the key word here is *simultaneously*. Power can be shared when it does not compete for the same resource at the same time. Many less successful RMs are unaware of this principle of the power game. They seek to obtain all of the power all of the time (absolute power), which maximizes conflict; or they assume that existing power relationships tend to be unchangeable—in other words, they either give up or they attempt to get things done with insufficient power, thereby limiting their success.

Collectively, all of the available power (we are thinking of it here as the control of resources) can be found in the various formal and informal organizations within the overall organization. To use power effectively, the successful RM (like the one we quoted above) must acquire control of resources either by demanding them formally or by calling in favors informally. The ability to obtain such control without alienating informal colleagues or formal superiors is a significant litmus test: successful RMs are good at it, their less successful counterparts aren't. Our study verified this conclusion empirically by finding that successful RMs engaged in relatively more observed gamesmanship and, especially among higher-level RMs, managed conflict much more often and more effectively (for example, appealing to higher authority or third-party negotiators).

THE USE OF POWER: MAINTAINING A BALANCE

Successful RMs not only use power, they maintain a delicate balance between impotence and empire-building. In other words, they know when not to throw their weight around and when they need to be forceful. They are also selective about the amounts and kinds of power they acquire; thus, their leadership style is critical to their success.

Our observations of RMs fit with what management theorists have written about success. First, successful managers may be deeper thinkers than unsuccessful ones: theorists call this *cognitive complexity*. In short, cognitive complexity says that successful managers are more capable of dealing with the increasing complexity found in today's organizations. Second, management researchers have found that leaders are more intelligent than their followers, on average. Successful managers are better able to consider a broad array of facts and ever-increasing amounts of information as they develop effective strategies and tactics. Because they are good at this process, they can more easily obtain the power to make good decisions and get them implemented. All of this takes raw intelligence. One successful manager commented:

> *The main reason I feel I have been relatively successful around here is that I can do the simple things like read faster and remember better than my colleagues. For example, I sit on the finance committee. I have no trouble understanding or remembering the data that is constantly being thrown at us. Brad, on the other hand, just can't get it through his head. The boss, of course, notices this*

*also, and while I am getting excellent appraisals and am
due for a promotion, Brad is in trouble.*

Of course, intelligence is not just genetic: it can be cultivated as
well. That said, it is clear that managers who aren't constantly working
to improve their cognitive abilities will be less successful than those
who are—not to mention managers who bring a quick, organized
brain to the table in the first place.

Third, we noticed that most, if not all, successful managers share
a strong need for power. Managers express this hunger for power as
the need to be in charge, or the desire to manipulate others. Most of us
instinctively recoil from such a seemingly negative, self-serving need,
but there is actually a more neutral interpretation of it, as pioneering
Harvard psychologist David McClelland has described. He interprets
this need for power as having two dimensions, or "faces." The negative face is "personal power": manipulation and personal gain at the
expense of others. In contrast, he proposes another face he calls "social
power," which concentrates on helping the group get ahead. Crucially,
it places this group identity above the individual need: *"Our* department is going to be the best in the company," not "*I* am going to really
look good so *I* can get promoted."

In other words, social power needs are more concerned with the
kinds of goals managers set, and their effect on the self-esteem and
growth of subordinates. McClelland's evidence suggests that social-
power-motivated managers may be more effective than personal power types. However, those with intense personal power needs may be
more *successful*, especially if they keep mobile. One subordinate of a
personal-power-oriented manager commented:

> *He has been successful all right. He has always kept one
> step ahead of the wolves. The decisions he makes in our
> department make him look good in the eyes of upper
> management. But those of us who have to carry out his
> decisions know that they are really not the best for the
> goals of the company as a whole. I suppose it will only
> be a matter of time before he gets another big promotion
> and we will be left holding his bag of problems.*

This subordinate could hardly be clearer about the corrosive effects of the drive for individual power on effective management. In effect, his or her boss has achieved individual success by outrunning the pitchfork-wielding mob—not a recipe for effectiveness. This intriguing dichotomy helps explain why we found such a contrast between the high use of networking by successful RMs and its minimal use by effective RMs in our studies.

Yet, personal power may be a prerequisite to the maintenance and exercise of social power. In other words, it's possible that RMs must accumulate individual power before they can even have a chance to exercise broader organizational power. RMs should think of the exercise of individual power in this way: not as a zero-sum game, but as a beneficial practice that can be leveraged for the greater organizational good. In other words, as in the other dimensions of RMs, there is probably no "best" type of power. Each may be necessary, depending on the situation. Thinking of the exercise of power in this way is a route to combining success with effective management.

SOCIAL SKILLS FOR SUCCESS

> **Subordinate:** *He often has lunch with managers one and two levels above him. The conversations at those luncheons usually revolve around social issues and about what is going on in the department. He's greased the skids for me more than once. I owe him a lot.*

> **Colleague:** *He's got a lot of clout. He socializes with the powerful personalities in the company and with prominent community leaders outside the company. His position in the company isn't very high, but he seems to have formidable influence everywhere. I would hate to think of him as anything but a good friend when I need to get something done.*

The vital role played by individuals' need for power reflects another of our findings: Social skills are a more important ingredient in networking than even the power dynamics of the informal organization. Social skills are closely related to the socialization process and group dynamics, and managers who can't interact easily with individuals and groups are not likely to end up being successful at the organizational level. However, RMs with good social skills are also sensitive to the need for self-management, and they understand where their own perspective fits into the larger organizational whole.

Moreover, social skills are not permanent or fixed: like any set of skills, they can deteriorate with disuse and improve with practice. New managers thus tend to work hard to develop their social skills, recognizing how central that work is to their success. Conversely, managers in dead-end jobs, doing the same kind of work over a long period of time, are liable to become jaded about their own declining social skills.

One of our RMs, approaching retirement age at the time of the study, gave us an object lesson in this deterioration as he related the course of his career. He was a hard worker all his life and, as many RMs do, translated his personal experience and beliefs about work into something like a religion. His beliefs were so firm and structured that he regarded those who had differing work-related views with contempt. This manager was not very successful (in terms of the definition we used in our study), although he had reached a fairly high level because of his long seniority. Because of his drive and capacity for hard work, he had been a very successful middle manager early on.

Later in his career, however, he grew intolerant of those with less drive and experience. When his subordinates or peers disagreed with him, or when they made constructive suggestions, he often responded with anger and abusive language. Consequently, although he was entrenched (and could not realistically be fired), he became an organizational pariah. This manager had had a heart attack, and, stressful as his work life was, the human resources director was worried he might not survive a second.

Incredibly, the RM saw it just the same way. He told us he had substantial income-producing agricultural property and didn't really need the job, but he regarded compromise as a threat to the power he had worked so hard to attain. He felt alienated and isolated; he was "surrounded by enemies" who were "out to get him." He really wanted to retire to lead a more relaxed life on his farm. Obviously, he needed professional help, but he refused to seek it out. Finally, the HR manager ordered him to get the help he needed, on medical grounds; if he didn't, he'd forfeit his retirement and survivor benefits. Several months later, he retired voluntarily.

This RM couldn't get along with anyone, and isolated himself as a result. His example illustrates the close relationship between social skills and support networks. Towards the end of his career, unable to interact with his coworkers, he operated within a rigid interpersonal structure of his own creation. His dogmatic approach denied him any reciprocal social influence; needing a social support network to succeed as a manager (indeed, given his medical history, for his very survival), he had ironically closed off all avenues to building one.

No longer able to compromise, this manager had backed himself into an almost inescapable corner. From his perspective, he couldn't accept the fact that he lacked sufficient social skills to get along with anyone—up, down, or horizontally. As long as he believed that his retirement benefits would accrue to his survivors, he didn't even care if he died as a result of the conflict and stress he had helped to create. The HR director, on the other hand, was more socially skillful. She used and enlarged her social skills in trying to solve this difficult personnel problem to benefit herself, the organization, and the ailing manager.

POLITICAL SKILLS FOR SUCCESS

Political skills are closely related to social skills. Politics, like power, often has negative connotations, but when we say "politics" and "political skills," we mean the practice of guiding and influencing organizational outcomes to one's own ends. Politics does not necessarily involve cunning or dishonest influence. In business and other organizations, we view political skills as just another tool in the RM's kit.

RMs have many different political skills and strategies at their disposal, all of which can potentially further their success. Their political choices depend on the information and resources available to them from their networking connections. In effect, political skills activate and actualize the potential of networks. Here is a sampling of some commonly used political strategies found in the literature employed by successful RMs, in conjunction with their networking activities:

1. *Divide and rule.* Those who are divided may choose to form their own networks. When an informal network has competing

and irreconcilable goals, breaking it into separate groups might be the only way to successfully activate it.

2. *Maintain alliances with powerful people.* This includes networking with members of important departments, strategically placed secretaries, staff assistants, or anyone close to powerful people. Judicious politicking with those in power activates the links between formal and informal networks.

3. *Embrace or demolish.* When a new manager takes over an organization, high-level managers should be either warmly welcomed or terminated. If they are downgraded and retained, they will remain determined to recover their lost power. If so, the information afforded through networking is essential for the new manager to be effective.

4. *Collect and use IOUs.* This strategy is an integral part of networking. Failing to pay IOUs when called due adversely affects both membership in networks and the attainment of power in the organization. Once burned, twice shy: When an RM calls in her chits and her contact doesn't come through, that part of the network will probably lapse into inactivity. Here, more than in any other aspect of managerial success, there is no free lunch.

5. *Manipulate scarce information.* Information used as a commodity to gain power can be expanded by careful politicking. As the RM expands his networks, the sources of such information expand along with them.

6. *Make a quick showing.* An expansive network provides more than personal contacts; it also potentially provides access to a wide variety of physical and organizational resources. This can be a real advantage for an RM looking to impress on a task right away; she can more efficiently marshal supplementary resources, unavailable to her peers, that she gained through networking.

7. *Wait for a crisis.* Opportunities to develop and use political skills are often present when the organization is in trouble. During crises, programmed decision-making is relaxed and RMs who activate their networks can make impactful decisions that bend or even break the rules. This gives them greatly increased

opportunities for brilliant success—or ignominious failure. Crises create stark risk/reward scenarios.

8. *Avoid decisive engagement.* To use an evolutionary, rather than a revolutionary, approach and to avoid "ruffling feathers" requires reliable knowledge of the pitfalls to avoid. That knowledge, information almost never available through the formal organization, usually funnels only through networking channels.

9. *Progress gradually.* When contemplating organizational (and personal) advancement, seek a foothold by beginning with incremental, inconspicuous moves, then use those small changes as a basis for larger accomplishments. Networking provides the information to get this done discreetly.

In real life, individual political strategies like these interact with and influence each other in complex patterns, and RMs use combinations of them based on their power, social skills, and available information. An example will help illustrate the web of political strategy. In one organization we learned about during the study, when a male employee was promoted over two qualified female employees, the women decided to use political skills to address the issue. The women organized an after-work discussion group, inviting outsiders to talk about women's careers. Although bland on the surface, these meetings masked a deep political strategy: developing a shared belief that the career development of women in the company was arrested by a congenial, but chauvinist, HR manager. They were convinced that a formal confrontation would have produced much conflict, but little change. Instead, these women set out to change the manager's behavior systematically, slowly teasing him at first. In time, he recognized that he had been targeted and labeled. As a result, he really had no graceful alternative but to promote a qualified woman as soon as possible.

There are several important points here. First, this informal group recognized a common problem, then formed a network and developed a strategy to solve it. Second, the network had influence (power) that was otherwise unavailable to them as isolated individuals. And third, these women solved the problem, thanks to their political skills. The process worked beneficially in both directions; the informal organization's women achieved their goal (and probably set the stage for further progress), and the male manager got to show a progressive side and avoid potential trouble further down the line. Maybe he even learned something, despite himself!

NETWORKS FOR REAL MANAGERS

The socializing and politicking behaviors we observed among our most successful RMs are in some ways consistent with the traditional notion of success-oriented managers. In this case, theory and our study both jibe with common sense: Success-driven managers try to develop useful networks with people both inside and outside their work settings. Why, then, are some RMs more successful than others? Is it a matter of luck, or is something else involved? Even members of formal networks seem to experience varying degrees of career success. Let's take a look at some features of networks, and how they can lead to success for their members—or even make effective management easier.

Networks offer powerful influences for their members. Some formal networks have scheduled meetings, are visited by top-level management who provide useful information, and conduct activities targeted to individual career development. Large formal networks within individual organizations play a central part in this kind of organization-wide education and information dissemination. When they proliferate widely, such formal networks can affect things as basic as work assignments and promotion.

On the other hand, networks can harm an organization's cohesion by creating rifts between different groups of people. We might think of this as the "good old boy" syndrome. This can happen when a network emphasizes exclusivity instead of inclusion and benefits to the larger organization—success instead of effectiveness, in other words. For example, one formal network we have seen in our research, which became a company-sanctioned group and grew tenfold during a ten-year period, had no legitimate (official) power in the formal organization. It accumulated power instead as an informal network, which influenced employee attitudes and affected company policies; in sum, it shaped organizational culture. Consequently, members of the network shared more power in the organization than did nonmembers. This suggested to us a form of "unionism," which is *decidedly not* the purpose of networking. In other words, successful RMs tend to rely too heavily on the power of membership in the network *per se*, rather than on the productive use of the network to get the job done and accomplish performance goals.

With all the publicity given formal networks, and with the stereotype of the old boy network, it isn't surprising that some RMs are misled into believing that membership is all that is required. It's easy to overlook the "exchange ratio": the proportion of networking inputs versus operational outcomes for the Real Manager. Membership in a network is no insurance against exploitation of either the member or the network. Just as many of us have difficulty translating theory into practice, membership in a network, either formal or informal, is of little value if it cannot be translated into performance.

However, if they are willing to move beyond back-slapping and glad-handing into networking connections that can really affect the bottom line, networks can provide RMs at all levels with information vital to their success. Effective networks help RMs answer important questions such as the following:

- Who has the final word on approvals?
- Who has the final word documenting a change?
- Who does one approach for restricted or confidential information?
- What strategies are most effective to get the job done in a visible way?
- How does one sell top-level management on proposed ideas or changes?
- Who controls the release of financial records for review?
- How does one obtain referrals to and from other network members?
- How and by whom is two-way feedback channeled?

All of these practices provide the structure for socializing and politicking. And through that process, as our study showed conclusively, networking enhances RMs' organizational success, as defined by the promotion index.

A more specific example illustrates the process: to get ahead, many RMs cultivate relationships with mentors as a powerful networking strategy. The mentor is usually a powerful manager who sponsors, formally or informally, one of their subordinates—a protégé. In the process, the protégé acquires a teacher, psychological and social support, confidence, career guidance, access to resources, a degree of protection, and an advocate. Mentors benefit too: with task-oriented help, new information, loyal followers and associates, expansion of their power base, and a reputation as a star-maker and the prestige that comes with reputation. In other words, mentoring is a win-win.

However, as in all networking, mentoring entails certain risks and costs. For one thing, it takes time: time to develop a network of obligations owed to you, and time to reciprocate favors. In addition, the protégé might fail, discrediting the mentor/protégé relationship. The ever-present risk of bringing an incompetent into the network means that, just as prestige is shared, failure and infamy is also shared. If the mentor risks choosing an incompetent protégé—one who develops into an embarrassment, an outcast, say—the protégé risks just as much, if for some reason the mentor becomes a pariah in the organization. Protégés and mentors are tarred with the same brush, just as they are put on the same pedestal.

However, despite the risks, it is very clear that RMs who network effectively tend to get ahead. But does this make them good managers? Turning this important result on its head, we can ask: are RMs who *network effectively* also *effective thanks to their networking?* Our study results indicated that the answer is no. Despite its many functional attributes for success in terms of getting ahead, networking may actually be harmful to effectiveness if the RM uses it in inappropriate situations. For instance, networking provides managers with friendly support that can be called upon in time of need or for getting ahead, but it does not excuse managers from doing their homework (for example, being prepared for a budget meeting). Being good at socializing, politicking, and interacting with outsiders only gets you so far.

In fact, the factors that make RMs good networkers are likely very similar to factors that affect organizational effectiveness in general. That is, managers who work for effective organizations tend to have more extensive and effective networks. These factors include: the amount of reciprocal trust among network members; the degree of interdependence among network members and how that interdependence is orchestrated; common goals among participants; and credibility and quality of resources. The effectiveness of networking may depend a great deal on credibility.

Here are some guidelines you can use to make networking more effective:

- Ask questions—don't make assumptions.
- Don't be bored—listen.
- Return favors promptly, in measure of quantity and quality.
- Don't lose contacts—follow up, keep in touch, report back.
- Be businesslike and professional in the network; satisfy personal and social needs elsewhere.
- Ask for what you need.
- Help others, be useful, and follow through.
- Be discreet—don't tell everything to everybody.
- Know your own limitations; don't expect miracles from others in the network.
- Conduct post mortems on your networking failures for clues to succeed in future attempts.

It is clear that networking influences both the hiring and turnover processes in today's organizations. Managers have always recognized the influence of networking on hiring; networks forge personal connections above and beyond an individual's qualifications. What might surprise readers is that research has shown that networking helps organizations retain employees longer. For example, studies have found a lower turnover rate among employees who knew people in the organization before they were hired than among those who didn't. Prospective employees with inside contacts have better, more, and more realistic information about their future jobs than people not so in the know.

Networking also tends to be self-reinforcing. Management researchers have found that people in positions of authority are connected to more network channels than are those with little or no authority, which certainly makes intuitive sense. This may sound like the classic chicken-and-egg question: Which came first, the authority or the contacts? Our study makes the answer clear: It's the hardworking RMs who cultivate those contacts from the beginning of their careers. Successful RMs do more networking activity, acquire control of resources (power), and thus, are more likely to be sought after as connections.

Finally, much evidence, including our own studies, suggests that the long-term influence of networking is a reciprocal, interactive process between each member of the network and its related organizational and social context. Communication flows in a network go up, down, and sideways, they change over time, and they web the network into the larger group of people to whom the network belongs. In short, networks are flexible. They influence their members just as their members change the composition of networks, and they impact both social interactions and work processes.

There is evidence that the specific organizational situation helps determine and control the freedom of participants to change from one network to another, because social homogeneity (the fact that most people tend to think and behave alike) reduces uncertainty in the organization. While this is probably true when it comes to internal work activities, it may not hold up in the broader social context, since social networks cross organizational lines. In other words, it is virtually impossible to keep networks purely social or purely work related. Even professional, formally designated networks have inviolate social rules baked into them. This dynamic process profoundly affects outcomes such as promotions and career success.

Some obvious conclusions flow from the insights we've drawn from our study and detailed in this chapter. The most important may be that networking is the activity least strongly related to RM effectiveness. The consequences of this insight are profound: Managerial effectiveness is largely divorced from one of the most consequential activities that powerful, active managers engage in. The corollary to this is that networking is crucial to managerial *success*—to getting promoted and getting ahead. Networking taps the unique social and political skills of successful RMs, who thus do relatively more networking than their less successful counterparts. In short, networking is indispensable to RMs seeking to acquire and retain power.

CHAPTER **EIGHT**

Human Resource Management Activities

Subordinate: She's highly motivated herself, and it's infectious. Whenever an Emergency Code is well run on the floor and the doctors are complimentary, she always lets us know how pleased they are with us. What a contrast to her predecessor! She provided no feedback, had no incentive programs, and never praised anyone for a job well done.

Colleague: He fired a person on the spot for harassing another individual. He doesn't hesitate to give verbal reprimands. When he cannot tolerate continued activity or inactivity of any particular kind, he leaves no doubt about what he expects.

JUST LIKE COMMUNICATION AND NETWORKING, HUMAN resources activities show that managerial success and effectiveness are not always equally served by the same activities. We saw that networking makes the biggest contribution to success; human resources activities, on the other hand, make the smallest. Taking care of human resources tasks is not a recipe for getting ahead. However, like communication, human resources activities have a great deal to do with *effective* management. In fact, they make the second greatest contribution to effectiveness (after communication).

Our study once again demonstrated this gap between activities that contribute to success and those that generate effective management. Although the human resource management activities occurred with basically the same relative frequency as the other activities, they were last in relative strength of relationship in the success analysis. The comparative analysis found that the top third of successful RMs did about 25% less of these HR activities than did the bottom third. In the effectiveness analysis, however, these HR activities came in a strong second in terms of relative strength of relationship. As a rule of thumb, effective managers practice these activities; successful managers don't (see Figure 8-1).

FIGURE 8-1
Distribution of Human Resources Management Activities

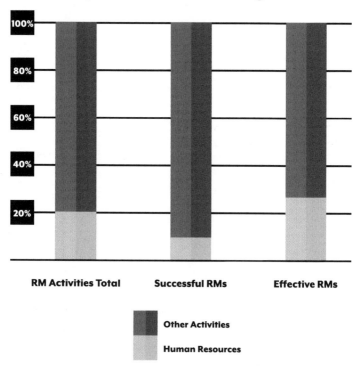

What exactly are these activities? Human resource management, by its very nature (and as defined in our study) is much more multidimensional than the other activities, so it would behoove the Real Manager to have a keen sense for the breadth of these activities, and, of course, their repercussions for success and effectiveness. We used the following behavioral categories in our study: *motivating/reinforcing, managing conflict, disciplining/punishing, staffing, and training/developing*. Table 8-1 lays out some actual examples drawn from our interviews. In the rest of the chapter, we examine these activities in greater depth and discuss the implications of them for RMs.

TABLE 8-1
*Human Resource Management Activities: Some Examples**

MOTIVATING/REINFORCING

HIGH AMOUNT	MEDIUM AMOUNT	LOW AMOUNT
Writes a letter about what a fine job the individual did and puts a copy into the person's personnel file.	Compliments employee for job well done in front of other managers.	Tells a subordinate in passing, "You did a good job."

DISCIPLINING/PUNISHING

HIGH AMOUNT	MEDIUM AMOUNT	LOW AMOUNT
Fires an individual for continually being late.	Writes a formal reprimand on a worker who is continually late and logs the reprimand in their personnel file.	Yells at a worker for continually being late.

MANAGING CONFLICT

HIGH AMOUNT	MEDIUM AMOUNT	LOW AMOUNT
Calls involved workers together and discusses the situation with them in an effort to arrive at a solution acceptable to all	Makes a decision regarding how to resolve the conflict and tells those involved what it is.	Separates those who are involved so that arguments and personal interaction are minimized.

STAFFING

HIGH AMOUNT	MEDIUM AMOUNT	LOW AMOUNT
Reviews all personnel records and conducts interviews among those who have applied for the job, then makes the hiring decision.	Sets Hiring criteria, reduces the list of candidates based on these criteria, and then makes a decision regarding whom to hire.	Uses hiring criteria to determine who is the best candidate and makes a decision as quickly as possible given this information.

TRAINING/DEVELOPING

HIGH AMOUNT	MEDIUM AMOUNT	LOW AMOUNT
Identifies training and development needs throughout the department or unit and then coordinates with the people who are responsible for providing this training	Personally determines the types of training and development that unit personnel need and sends this information to those who are responsible for providing the training.	Has personnel identify the types of training and development they feel they need and encourages them to attend seminars and programs that will provide it.

*These examples are drawn from structured interviews with RMs.

MOTIVATING AND REINFORCING

While motivation is a complex psychological process, we define it simply as a desire or need that drives someone toward a goal or incentive. For certain needs, such as achievement or self-esteem, the goal or the reward is often money, promotion, or recognition, but regardless of the motivational cause, behavior is still a function of its consequences. Put simply, if the consequence of your behavior as an RM reinforces that behavior, you will do it more afterwards. If you get punished for your behavior—say, chewed out, shifted to a less important project, or put on close supervision—you will do it less.

Motivation and reinforcement tie together a series of management activities. They begin with an RM's attempt to understand his or her people's needs; then, the RM attempts to fulfill those needs; finally, the RM reinforces behaviors that contribute to performance goals. The motivating and reinforcing behaviors we observed included: *providing increased job challenges and responsibilities, listening to suggestions, conveying appreciation and recognition, providing performance feedback, and allocating formal rewards.* As we examine each of these in turn, we provide representative accounts of how Real Managers actually carry out these motivating/reinforcing behaviors as part of their day-to-day human resource management activities.

Increasing Job Challenges

Sometimes, RMs realize that making their teams' jobs harder drives organizational success. In this sense, giving subordinates new challenges to attain difficult (but not impossible) goals and overcome obstacles is actually a motivational strategy. RMs can increase the challenge of their subordinates' jobs in a number of ways. They can, for example, empower their subordinates by allowing more authority to make decisions: in other words, increasing their autonomy. People tend to be motivated by jobs that offer them freedom, independence, and discretion in scheduling the work and determining how to most effectively carry it out. One manager commented:

> *My people don't need me looking over their shoulders every five minutes. What I do is tell them what needs to be done and when it should be accomplished. I don't*

*care how fast they work just as long as work is done on
time. If they want to take 20 minutes for coffee rather
than the usual 10 minutes, that's fine with me. They can
even go to lunch a little early. And if I see them in the cor-
ridor or in one another's office talking, I don't care. It's
up to them how they get the work done. My job is seeing
that it's done on time and done right. Aside from this, I
try to stay out of their way and not over-control the job.*

This RM realized that autonomy inheres not just in big decisions,
but in the small actions and transactions of the workday. These individuals and teams have more autonomy because the boss avoids the
little irritants that add up to low morale.

Effective RMs also increase job challenge by giving their people
the authority to control their own work. Instead of waiting for a sign-
off from outside the work group, individual employees and teams are
in charge of policing themselves. For example, if Group A is responsible for producing computer disk drives and Group B's job is to test
these drives, there is an inevitable conflict. Group B controls Group
A to the extent that Group B either passes or rejects Group A's work.
To overcome this potential problem, some RMs give their work groups
the equipment and authority to check their own work. In this way, the
group becomes accountable for its own output, and can fix or rework
subpar units. As part of this process, effective RMs reinforce the individual and the group with feedback and recognition (contingent on
the actual work, of course) for taking on the added responsibility and
correcting quality problems.

Effective RMs also find ways for people to realize the significance
of their own work; they not only help people see the big picture, they
also highlight their subordinates' role within it. Quite often, Real Managers discover that when their employees are aware of the important
role they play, they are more motivated and at least potentially more
effective. One manager in our study related an example:

*We often have customers come to the firm to see how
we build these units. Sometimes it's new customers, but
quite often they have been buying from us for the last
couple of years and we've invited them in as a public*

relations gesture. During these visits, I like to get some of the customers off to the side to visit with some of my people down on the line. I have the customer explain to them how important their work is from a safety standpoint. If one of these units is built wrong, a major accident could take place. Once my people realize how much others are depending on them to build the unit right, their motivation to produce a "no defects" product seems to go up.

Cleverly, the RM in this case created a way to reveal to his or her employees how important their jobs were through a proxy—the customer. Becoming aware of the importance of a safe product from customer feedback, instead of simply getting a directive from corporate, made it that much more significant.

Listening to Suggestions

Effective RMs listen to suggestions from their subordinates because it helps them do their job better. Of course, any manager knows it makes intuitive sense that, when solving problems or changing procedures, the employee on the assembly line or the salesperson in direct contact with the customer knows the best approach to use or the one solution that will work, but the most effective RMs know that listening can also be an important motivating/reinforcing tool. It has the potential to not only solve the problem, but motivate the subordinate to boot. One manager told us this story:

We had a problem meeting our department's standards. No matter how hard we tried, we always seemed to fall 10-15% short of the recognized standard. I called a meeting and asked everyone for suggestions about what we could do. A couple of the people pointed out that the time allocated for assembling the units was way too short. In particular, one of the parts was supposed to be installed in 55 seconds, but the fastest time they could get it done in was 85 seconds. The general manager sent down a design engineer and he checked the part against the blueprints. It was built exactly as called for in the specs. However, when we asked him to assemble it, it took the engineer over two minutes. The problem was that the part was too big and it had to be worked into the unit, rather than adjusted and then snapped in. The engineer redesigned the blueprint, and ever since, we've been able to meet the standard.

By listening carefully, this RM solved a small but important problem that impacted the department's overall performance. Undoubtedly, the line employees came away from the incident aware that their boss valued their expertise.

We talked about active listening in the last chapter; it's an important technique in human resources as well. Active listening involves letting the other person talk without giving any direction or advice. During active listening, the RM should seek clarification or extension of the explanation, rather than jumping in too quickly to offer guidance or support. Language like, "You seem quite upset over this matter," "I see," and "What else?" urges your interlocutor away from preparing a response to your order or opinion and toward opening up fully about the issue. Such language also reveals information and possible avenues towards a solution. The objective is to keep the other person talking. But in addition to getting information, this approach can be cathartic for the speaker. It is particularly useful in motivating/reinforcing subordinates who are upset over some event and want their boss to know about it. For example, a manager related an incident following their company's decision to end overtime:

When Greg came in here, he was really mad. He felt his people relied heavily on overtime to supplement their base pay and he felt that management's decision was going to wreak havoc on his people. I just let him talk. He had a right to be angry. Top management had often pointed out that because of overtime we were able to pay higher annual take-home pay than anyone else in the local area. They really were pushing overtime as a part of the total compensation package. When management suddenly cut it out because of a supposed downturn in sales, we were all shocked. When Greg finished, we just sat here and looked at each other for a couple of minutes. Then he got up and said, "Thanks for listening," went back to his office, and that was it. I later heard he called his people together, backed management to the hilt, and told them that the company had been good to them over the years and they should be thankful that overtime had lasted this long. His unit is still one of the best we've got.

Active listening—in this case, just sitting and agreeing, "You're right, that's terrible,"—created such strong motivation that the employees went against their own self-interest and backed management in their salary cut.

Few things feel as good as getting heartfelt, genuine praise and recognition from your boss. RMs should cultivate the skill of positive reinforcement, and luckily there are all sorts of ways to do this. Behind all of them is the simple fact that conveying appreciation and recognition to your subordinates and direct reports, no matter how you do it, motivates them. One employee we interviewed put it simply:

He tells me when I'm doing well, and he tells higher-level management when I'm doing well. I know this because they come to me to congratulate me for good progress on a given project. He even remembers birthdays and holidays. He's got an informal incentive program where the best performer for the month is designated "star of the month" and is invited to a free lunch.

Besides recognizing and praising the employee in several different ways, note that this RM made sure to go up a level or two by bringing the employee's good work to the attention of upper management, and telling the employee about it—surely one of the best kinds of official praise.

The RM above also mixed two streams of praise: verbal and written. Both of these practices are important components of appreciation and recognition. Verbal appreciation usually happens on a face-to-face basis: "You did a nice job on the industrial products account"; "I saw your monthly sales projections and you're doing great work"; and "Nice going. That last monthly report you submitted was excellent."

Managers use verbal praise more widely than written because it is easier to provide and can be used in reinforcing any type of performance:
from lackluster but improving ("You're really getting a lot better."),
to outstanding ("Your sales are the highest we've ever had in a three-
month period!"). Many effective RMs use verbal reinforcement on a
day-to-day basis to foster motivation, often through their own version
of management-by-walking-around. One effective manager described
such a technique to us:

> *Every day I make it a point to look at performance data
> from the day before. In this way, I know how well each
> of my people are doing. This is important if I'm going to
> get out there and reinforce them on a daily basis. Once
> I've reviewed the data, I begin making my daily rounds.
> Those who have done a good job hear about it from me.
> Those who haven't are offered encouragement—unless
> their performance has been down for three to four days.
> Then I make it a point to call them over to the side and
> talk with them and offer my help to get them back on
> track. You know what? My people like the fact that I
> know how well they're doing. They know I wouldn't pay
> attention if I didn't care.*

This RM made his motivational activity more effective by doing
it in person and orally; he walked around encouraging and cajoling
instead of writing an email or text message. This provided a constant
stream of memorable reinforcement to his team.

Written recognition, more formal than verbal, can also be powerful, however; when merited, it's a good idea to put your praise and
recognition in writing, especially if it reinforces verbal praise. Many
effective RMs use written recognition as documentation for the individual's personnel file, but its beneficial effects go far beyond just
recording good work. For example, in one case an RM reported that
three of her people had developed a new major cost-saving suggestion. The company gave each of these individuals a financial reward
for the suggestion. However, the RM went further and sent each a personal memo relating how important their suggestion had been and
praising them for it. A copy of the memo was put into each of their

personnel files. Two kinds of written recognition, an official report and a personal note (both lodged in the employees' personnel files) made their work seem that much more impactful—not to mention the financial reward! Recognition and praise often act as particularly inspirational performance feedback.

Of course, official performance feedback is one of the most powerful ways that effective RMs can reinforce and motivate their people. All RMs can give their teams effective performance feedback; feedback that is, we like to say, PIGS. (Hear us out.) First, feedback should be positive. People do not like to listen to negative feedback; they tune it out. RMs should make every attempt to convey even bad news in as positive a light as possible. Second, the feedback should be immediate or be given as soon as possible. Third, if possible, the feedback should be presented graphically rather than numerically—think a colorful chart or graph instead of columns of numbers. People get more information more quickly from a graph, and they understand the significance of the information more fully. One manager used this feedback method:

> *The accounting people provide us with these neatly bound figures every quarter. Frankly, I have trouble figuring them out myself, let alone passing this data on down to my people, so the reports just accumulate over in the corner there. Lately, though, I have been posting our weekly production figures on a graph. I personally keep it up to date, on the wall of our employee lounge. I see them gather around this graph all the time and they seem to know where we stand. The productivity rate has definitely gone up since I started doing this. 1 can show you the graph to prove it to you.*

Finally, the feedback should be as *specific* as possible. If it can be quantified, it should be.

Table 8-2 depicts such PIGS feedback.

TABLE 8-2
"PIGS" Feedback.

POSITIVE	Feedback has to be positive; people will not listen to negative feedback. There is a positive and negative side to everything. Talk about uptime rather than downtime, attendance rather than absenteeism, retention rather than turnover, approach goals (10% improvement) rather than avoidance goals (10% fewer rejects).
IMMEDIATE	Real time feedback is the best—the sooner the better. Quarterly reports and annual performance appraisals are not sufficient. Ideally, feedback should happen at the same time as the behavior itself, as in some jobs such as face-to-face sales and in self-feedback systems. If not simultaneously, then give feedback hourly, daily, or in some cases, weekly, but don't wait longer than that.
GRAPHIC	Feedback should be visual. Tables of figures do little to motivate and reinforce behavior. Instead, put the data into a graph whenever possible. This gives the employee an instant look at past, present, and future trends in a memorable format (e.g., the old sales chart). A single graph is worth a hundred pages of numbers.
SPECIFIC	The feedback should be as specific as possible. Quantify it as much as possible, and state it in relation to a goal. Relate it to the individual's job and performance, not their personality.

Words of recognition and encouragement, whether in verbal or written form, motivate employees to be their best, but eventually the rubber has to meet the road, and there has to be a tangible prize for finishing the obstacle course of hard work. The most obvious and permanent way to motivate people is the allocation of formal rewards—in other words, pay and promotion. Let's start with pay, which takes two general forms: across-the-board salary increases and merit pay. Across-the-board pay increases are given to everyone: for example, a company might give a 5% increase to all middle managers and supervisors, and 4% to all hourly employees. Such a raise has limited reinforcing/motivating value, because it does not consider performance. Everyone gets the same, whether they are effective or not. Merit pay, on the other hand, requires RMs' judgment, appraisal, and fairness, since they allocate discretionary funds based upon individual performance: for example, 8% for the best employees, 4% for average employees, and nothing for everyone else. Unfortunately, most organizations make heaviest use of across-the-board increases, especially in times of limited pay raises.

Many RMs in our study expressed little support for merit pay because it often involves giving a lot of money to a small percentage of employees and very little to the rest. More fundamentally, merit pay decisions demand that RMs track performance, justify their salary decisions to the organization, and explain them to the individuals involved. These are all demanding tasks that require the manager's careful input and leadership, and commitment from the organization. As a result, most organizations today have adopted an easier combination approach, allocating most of the money for across-the-board raises and a small percentage for merit.

The biggest problem with this mixed approach is that high performers tend to receive very little extra for their efforts. This reduces their motivation to maintain such a high level of output. High performers can be motivated in other ways to close this gap, like the nature of the work itself (that is, by making the work interesting and challenging). But formal rewards are the most direct approach, to the extent that the RM is able to tie pay to performance. Pay will always be a motivator.

In many cases, an organization can sidestep the across-the-board vs. merit pay dilemma by simply promoting deserving individuals and giving them the higher pay that goes along with the new position. To the extent that people desire promotion, this is an effective motivation/reinforcement strategy. However, it must be closely aligned with careful training and development (which we will discuss later in this chapter), to ensure that the individual is not pushed ahead too fast. Effective RMs recognize that some individuals do not want to be promoted and doing so results in problems for both the person and the organization. Our study turned up a good example of this dilemma:

> *Every year I recommend my two best people for promotions. Since we promote from within, both are usually moved up within a three-to-six-month time period. There's a lot of upward mobility around here because we have been expanding so quickly. However, I always make it a point to talk to my people before recommending them for anything. I learned this lesson the hard way. A few years back I strongly recommended a person who*

turned out to be a real dud. Not even extra training and development could help him. Why? Because he simply didn't want to be a manager. He liked working where he was and felt threatened by the increased responsibility. I made the mistake of thinking that a promotion is an important motivator without considering the individual's personal desires. For some people, doing things they're good at is more important than moving on to increased responsibilities and managing others.

RMs can't count on the tangibles of pay and promotion to satisfy everyone's desire for workplace fulfillment; it's rather a blunt instrument. This RM learned through experience that job satisfaction and using one's strengths runs deeper than power and even money.

DISCIPLINING AND PUNISHING

Nobody likes to punish their employees. In fact, we saw so few disciplining and punishing incidents in our study that we dropped the category from our analysis of successful and effective RMs. Nevertheless, discipline remains an important and sometimes necessary dimension of human resource management activities. Our key insight for effective RMs is that there is a fine line between discipline and punishment. Just as it is questionable that motivation and reinforcement can or should be categorized together, we should also recognize that there are key differences between effective discipline and dysfunctional punishment.

Discipline does not always have to be punitive. This insight reveals the first key difference between discipline and punishment: the end goal. Effective managers use discipline to prevent counterproductive behaviors from occurring in the future. Through positive discipline, RMs try to cultivate the right behaviors; that's the end goal of discipline. Punishment, on the other hand, often becomes an end in itself: the end goal of punishment is... to punish. It's true that, carefully and contingently administered, punishment can decrease the frequency of subsequent behavior. But herein lies the second key difference between positive discipline and punishment. As a method of human resource management, punishment tends to change or suppress counterproductive behavior only temporarily, and it tends to generate such undesirable side effects (like hate and revenge) that it's often self-defeating. Positive discipline, on the other hand, is preventative; it can change behavior permanently. It also minimizes the side-effect problems of punishment. Because its end goal focuses on changing counterproductive behavior with an eye toward the bottom line, instead of attacking the individual and his or her self-worth, positive discipline not only benefits the employee, it makes the RM better at his or her job. What are some specific discipline strategies that work toward this dual goal? Let's take a look at two that we saw in our study, which we might label *little by little* and *room for adjustment.*

The *little by little* strategy, more formally called progressive discipline, employs a series of escalating disciplinary steps or actions. Most effective, positive disciplinary processes use some form of it. It usually begins with an oral warning. If this corrects the problem, the effective RM stops there. If it doesn't, the RM takes a second disciplinary step, more severe than the first. If the pattern of misbehavior or error continues, the effective RM begins applying more and more sanctions until the employee is given the final disciplinary action—dismissal. A typical pattern of progressive discipline used by many organizations has four phases: an oral warning; a written warning, which is placed in the individual's personnel file; a disciplinary layoff (this will vary in length from one day to two weeks, depending on the nature of the problem); and, finally, discharge.

This is only one pattern of discipline. Realistically, especially in unionized firms, RMs may be unable to fire a person without collecting considerable hard evidence to back up their charge. Even then, it may be necessary to submit the entire matter to arbitration. Nevertheless, no matter how it's set up, the progressive discipline process has five distinguishing characteristics which establish the parameters surrounding the specific strategy. Each is important to effective RMs in their administration of discipline.

First, *discipline should be immediate,* following right after the effective RM checks the facts and knows that a rule or policy has been clearly violated. This immediacy establishes a causal link between the act and the discipline. Waiting to take disciplinary action only weakens this linkage. Second, *there should be advance warning of unambiguous activities that will elicit discipline.* Rules and policies should be made clear to all employees, and they should know what the penalties are for breaking them. If there is an orientation period for new employees, this information should be disseminated and explained at that time. *Third, rules should be kept to a minimum.* People tend to remember and follow only a few rules; when there are too many, violations increase. In organizations with a maze of complicated rules, employees simply cannot remember them all and, because there are so many, they tend to believe that none of them are really important. Fourth, *discipline should be consistent.* Individuals who commit the same offense should be given the same discipline—no playing favorites. Because everyone has had advance warning and knows the rules, penalties should be consistent from one person to the next. Finally, *discipline should be impersonal.* Everyone should be treated equally from the shop steward to the operating employee to the president's secretary. It's like the adage about the hot stove: the red stove gives a warning, but when it's touched everyone gets burned. Again, the RM can't have favorites, no matter who they are or what position they hold.

Sometimes punitive action is necessary, but only as a last resort. Effective RMs leave a window at the end of the process for their subordinate to change their behavior. We call this the *room-for-adjustment* strategy. First, RMs clarify *why* the action is being taken. Second, they clearly tie the punishment to the rule violation. Third, they give the person being punished a chance to modify or change their behavior and thus avoid future action. One RM's subordinate described this process in action in our study: "before he fired him, he brought the subordinate to his office, told him what he was doing wrong and how he wanted it done, and then gave him a chance to do it correctly. When the subordinate continued to do it wrong, he replaced him." Giving your subordinate a chance to adjust his behavior makes the punishment process easier for everyone involved—and more effective. Here is how one of our study participants described it:

> *Taking punitive action against one of my people is no fun. I really hate it. But it has to be done from time to time, if only to show the others that proper behavior is expected. Whenever I have to do this, there is one rule I always follow: Let the person know what was wrong*

*and how this can be avoided in the future. I never just
tell someone that he's done something wrong, lower the
boom on him, and walk away. I always come back at
the first opportunity and tell the person punished when
they did it right. This seems to help and they don't hold
a grudge or feel they have to get back at me somehow.*

By carefully explaining the chain of events, then giving his or her subordinate room to adjust, and finally dispensing more feedback and reinforcement when the subordinate acted correctly, this RM created a positive way forward to better behavior.

MANAGING CONFLICT

Effective RMs, as we have seen, have to manage their own and their employees' behavior in order to attain satisfaction and performance. They do this through motivating and reinforcing behaviors, and, if necessary, through positive discipline. All this relies heavily on effective communication, as we described in Chapter Six. But what happens when there is a conflict within or between teams? Just disciplining everyone is a recipe for disaster, and motivation won't remove the underlying conflict. Managing conflict among individuals and groups of people is an essential human resources activity for effective RMs.

The root causes of individual, group and organizational conflict are complex, and the effective RM should be aware of some of the reasons for them, apart from simple personality clashes. In organizational history, one of the most common causes of conflict is the lack of resources and the competition for them. For example, an organization that is working out next year's budget is likely to find that the requests of the major department heads are greater than the total amount available. Some (if not all) of the department heads are going to get less than they requested, and they will jockey for position and campaign to improve their chances for the largest relative share of the budgetary allocations. The savvy managers will compile data to show the positive effect of giving their department its request, and the negative effect of cutting this amount. Inevitably, some departments lose, others win—a zero-sum game. Obviously, the budgetary battle itself can be a bare-knuckle fight, and it's likely there will be conflict afterwards as well.

Unionization is another common source of conflict: it tends to foster an adversarial union-management relationship. Each side often tries to discredit the other or prevent it from attaining its objectives. Finally, we cannot discount the personality issue; sometimes individuals or groups simply don't like each other. These kinds of inter-individual or intra-group conflicts occur when superior/subordinate pairs or members of a department group are unable to get along with each other. Quite often the departments or conflicting parties involved undermine one another's efforts, to the detriment of the organization.

RMs have at their disposal a number of approaches to manage conflict. We focus on three: *cooperation and co-optation; appeals to higher authority;* and *third-party negotiation.* Mastering these conflict management tools is essential for the effective RM engaged in human resource management. Let's look at each in turn.

Probably the most common way for effective RMs to manage conflict is to seek *cooperation* among the conflicting parties. The RM can try to have the conflicting parties put aside their differences and focus on the overall objective; this is simple persuasion. If they already preside over a reasonably effective and harmonious team, the effective RM might be able to solve the conflict at this point. But again, this requires a manager who already exerts significant control over his team and its individual members, and a team that in turn trusts their manager. It is seldom this easy. Usually, conflict requires the RM to take some kind of action. This involves a bit of skill: effective RMs try to diagnose the real problem and then restructure the situation to reduce or eliminate the friction points that are causing the conflict. One manager told us how this works:

> *I found that about half the members of the department were upset with the other half. I really don't know how long this infighting had been going on; I guess for a couple of years before I got here. I know that both factions got along fine with their own members, but there was friction whenever cooperation between them was needed. I reorganized the unit and split it into two completely different parts. Now each group works independently*

of the other and productivity is higher than it has ever been. I know this isn't necessarily the ideal solution, but it took care of our problem, at least for the time being.

This RM obviously knew the organization inside and out. Through reorganization, she was able to mobilize greater productivity. Note that this RM was fully aware that the solution was not ideal, but she was comfortable with finding the rough-and-ready solution to jump-start productivity.

Ideally, the parties in the conflict will get involved themselves in finding a solution. We call this unknowingly forced involvement *co-optation.* Co-optation combines several strategies of the effective RM; it's a way to manage conflict, but it also involves active listening and reinforcing the right kind of workplace behaviors. The ability to guide employees toward solving their conflict is a key sign of an effective RM, because he is leading a team that, ultimately, trust each other. The strategy is particularly effective when those causing the conflict are interested in doing a good job but feel that the organization or their manager is ignoring them. One Real Manager gave us this example:

Every month we would get our computer printouts and use them to evaluate progress in the various units. Every month four of the supervisors in our group would complain that the printouts did not provide them with the right kinds of information for controlling operations. I got pretty steamed up after a while and said, "Okay, if you want a different type of printout, you design it. I'm appointing you as a committee of four. Go out to the field, find out what kinds of information we should be getting from those units, and coordinate your efforts with the computer staff to design and implement a system that will do what you think needs to be done." I didn't hear any more griping for the next two weeks. However, when the group came in with its revised form, I had to admit it was a lot better than what we had been using. They were right with their complaints. Today, we're much better able to monitor our field units than we were a year ago.

Cooptation is a powerful strategy, potent enough that, in this instance, the RM succeeded in managing conflict almost despite himself. He ignored the entreaties of his employees, then, "after a while," lost his temper and curtly ordered his team to find a better solution. They did. Just imagine what an effective RM, schooled in active listening and able to keep his temper, can accomplish by co-opting the energies and talents of his subordinates—his human resources!

Both cooperation and co-optation keep it in the family, so to speak; these strategies concentrate on problem-solving individually or within the workgroup. What happens, though, when nothing is working—when the family squabble is just too venomous or deeply seated? Sometimes conflict is so bad that it cannot be handled firsthand by the manager, and higher management has to step in. This is the *appeal to higher authority*. It is particularly common when managers are new at their jobs and their subordinates have been around for quite a while; the greenhorn manager has not yet gained the trust and respect of their people. Experienced subordinates tend to refuse to accept the authority of a new manager, no matter how hard the new RM tries.

One of the RMs in our study illustrated this difficulty, while pointedly highlighting the role gender can still play in RM/subordinate power games:

> When I took over I was the first woman manager they ever had around here. Everyone regarded me as nothing more than a token to help our EEO statistics. As a result, when I found that two of my experienced people were squabbling over some petty matter and called them in and told them to start cooperating, I couldn't get anywhere with them. However, this didn't last long. I explained the situation to my boss and he backed me up. He called both of these people into his office and spelled out the rules for them. This not only got me through my authority crisis in the department, but it handled the conflict problems as well. I'll admit that I haven't gone back for help since—but if I need it, I, and my people, know it's there.

This RM at least tried to induce cooperation (perhaps not very effectively, since she just "told them" to cooperate with each other). When that didn't work, she called in her boss—an example, in this case, of effective upward communication. Higher management didn't hesitate; the big boss laid down the law to the squabbling employees. While it is certainly better for morale when an RM is able to induce cooperation or cooptation on their own, sometimes an appeal to higher management is legitimately necessary.

If cooperation/co-optation and the appeal to higher authority are on opposite ends of the conflict management spectrum, *third-party mediation* falls somewhere in between them. In third-party mediation, the RM brings in someone from outside the workgroup or organization who has no direct authority to make the parties in the conflict do anything. The role of the third party (it may be simply a neutral person inside the organization, or a total outsider with mediation skills) is to influence, persuade, or negotiate between the sides, not to order or coerce the conflicting parties. For example: an RM couldn't get sufficient cooperation from two of his operating employees in a union shop. This RM—an effective one—didn't want to write them up or otherwise discipline them. Instead, he brought in the shop steward as a mediator. The steward talked to both workers and that was the end of it. Here's another example, from a different setting, of the effective use of a mutually respected third party:

> *I had some people in my department who were upset because we had installed computer equipment without consulting them. They complained that the equipment was too difficult to operate and they didn't understand the programs they were supposed to be using. I'll bet my junior high school child could have understood that material. These people just didn't want to learn how to use the machine. I handled the situation in two simple steps.*
>
> *First, I told them that this was a vital part of their job and they had to learn it. Second, I sent over the one person in the department who knew the hardware and software inside and out. She was definitely someone*

they all respected. It took only two days before these people were handling the computer and its programs as if they were born to the job.

If we believe the RM, the software in question was relatively easy to learn; her employees were just upset with the change to their job and how it was handled. The RM could perhaps have handled the change better; for example, she could have co-opted her employees by giving them a chance to comment on and even lead the installation. In any event, once the squabble was there (possibly the result of poor decisions on the RM's part) the RM did the right thing. Recognizing the intractability of the situation, she called in an outside mediator respected by both sides. Problem solved, and quickly.

STAFFING

Effective human resource management starts with the initial hire. Although often the province of the human resources department, staffing is one of the most important human resource management activities for all RMs because it sets the stage for the future effectiveness or failure of their units. Staffing, as one RM told us, can be a full-time headache even for managers outside the selection experts in the HR department:

I have to find candidates for openings, by advertising and by word-of-mouth. I always have to check the most current Equal Employment Opportunity regulations to keep out of trouble. I'm constantly planning for future personnel moves and trying to replace people we lose with little or no notice. Recruiting and hiring people to get the work done around here is a continuing challenge.

Effective RMs don't skimp on the process when they have a staffing need; they give their full attention to a series of specific functions, including developing job descriptions, interviewing candidates, and making the final staffing decision. Hiring the right people means less time spent on the other human resources activities. It also means that motivation will be more impactful, discipline will be milder, and conflicts will be relatively few and far between.

Job descriptions provide an important basis from which to make staffing decisions. If properly detailed, they include a general description of the job, examples of work performed, and the general qualification requirements that must be possessed by the prospective employee. A job description should be complete, listing all the activities carried out by the jobholder. The description must be carefully organized and clearly phrased, so that prospective employees understand the job's activities and the qualifications necessary to do them. The description should also be as concise as possible, providing brief examples of the work and specific job objectives that explain how their work will be measured. Although RMs usually do not actually write these descriptions, effective ones do ensure that they are sufficiently detailed and accurate to allow an easy preliminary screening of applicants.

Effective RMs like to talk to prospective job candidates before they are hired. Interviewing, the second link in the staffing chain, takes a number of different forms. Some RMs prefer a highly structured interview where they ask a series of preplanned questions. Others prefer unstructured interviews in which the manager and applicant casually talk and the RM tries to formulate an impression about the ability of the candidate to do the job. In both cases, the pre-interview staffing activities (writing the job description, recruiting candidates, and so forth) lead directly to a successful interview process, as this RM's experience demonstrated:

> When I hired an attorney for the company, it was a very long, involved, and careful process. Our executive committee listed the attorney's duties and I designed a profile. We contract with a selection firm that recruits, tests, and pre-screens salaried employees for us. When this company found likely candidates, I flew to other cities to interview them and narrowed the field to four. Then I invited them to the home office to interview with the rest of the staff.

Note the detailed groundwork this RM did in advance: writing the job description, engaging outside help, and winnowing the field through preliminary interviews. All that happened before the candidates even set foot in the RM's office.

The most common type of interview used by effective RMs has a combination structured/unstructured format. Formulating questions in advance ensures that no important ones go unasked, but committing at the same time to some unstructured back-and-forth leaves room for the candidate to show off their creativity and initiative. If more than one person is going to be interviewing the candidate, the effective RM coordinates this activity and works out in advance what each person will discuss with the candidate. In this way, interviewers don't ask the same questions over and over. When the interviews are finished, the questioners can pool their thoughts and provide the best possible judgment for the final staffing decision.

Effective RMs, in conjunction with the personnel department, formulate selection criteria and use these as guides in making the final staffing decision. They detail some of these criteria in the job description: formal education, experience, and so forth. Managers determine other measures on the basis of the interview or background checks: questions such as: How well does this individual work with others?; What are his or her goals?; and Will the person fit in well in this organization? Quite often these are judgment calls, but if they've put the proper hiring criteria in place, the RM should find it easier to make an informed decision. Through such a careful process, one effective manager was able to trust his intuition in the hiring process:

> *Before I hire, I like to talk to the applicant and get an idea of what this person is like. I think I know the type of person who will fit in here. I look for the right chemistry. If it's there, I hire the person; if it's not, I don't. This may sound awfully unsophisticated, but I look to the first part of the hiring process to handle the routine stuff such as experience, training, education, background, and so forth. All of this can be put down on a piece of paper and used to guide me. However, my hiring decision is based heavily on what isn't on the piece of paper.*

Because this RM was attentive to the entire staffing process, he was able to let intuition guide him at the end. In other words, care taken early in the process to find good prospective candidates gives the

RM the freedom to exercise their judgment, guided by experience, to choose amongst a field of good prospects.

TRAINING AND DEVELOPMENT

Training and development links the staffing function to all the other human resource management activities; it is the bridge that molds new hires into effective employees. Formal training and development, like staffing, is closely associated with the human resources department, but there are a number of activities that effective RMs carry out in this area. These range from the new hire's initial experience inside the organization—orientation—through to identifying training needs and providing on-the-job mentoring, and, for experienced employees, continuing education and development.

Orientation, that first experience for new employees, has too often been overlooked, but has very important long-run payoffs. In particular, some organizations have found that new personnel who don't get a realistic orientation are much more likely to leave during the first year than those who do. The orientation is the beginning, and therefore, the most important part of the socialization process for employees. The longer, more intense, and more realistic the orientation, the greater the chance that the new employee will learn the values and overall culture of the organization. One RM in our study lamented the lack of orientation when he was hired:

> We don't have formal training here. When I started, I received no training. Each of us was turned loose and we were expected to train ourselves. I expected some kind of formal orientation as a minimum for training, but even that wasn't provided. It's strange, because the boss says that formal training is an unnecessary expense to the company, but he spends a lot of his own time developing the people around him.

This RM's company skipped the orientation process, and as a result, its managers had to spend much extra time training and developing their unprepared and un-socialized employees. The supposedly "unnecessary expense" of orientation, in this RM's telling, hamstrung the effectiveness of the organization.

Orientations cover a broad range of topics, such as: the history of the organization and the major services or products it provides; its structure and reporting relationships; personnel rules, policies, and practices; compensation and benefits; and daily routines and regulations. In large organizations, the personnel department usually carries out the formal part of this orientation; in small organizations, the manager may handle this entire function. However, even in big organizations, RMs are largely responsible for instilling the organization's values and expectations in new employees under their direction, as well as guiding them through the organization's particular culture. Here are some guidelines for combining the formal and informal functions of the orientation:

- Orientation should start with the most relevant and useful kinds of information, and then proceed to the more general organizational context, and to peripheral details.
- A large percentage of the orientation should focus on: the socialization process, by providing information about supervisors and co-workers; how to get to the desired work output standards; and encouragement to seek advice and help when they are unsure of how to proceed with a work project.
- Each new employee (at all levels) should be assigned an experienced person—a mentor—who can provide assistance and encouragement, answer questions, and help the individual get through the first couple of months. This is vital to the employee's socialization process.
- New workers should be given sufficient time to master their jobs before the demands on them are increased; they should progress a step at a time.

Once recent hires have been oriented to their new organization, managers should identify further job-specific training needs and design the training to meet these needs. For new hires, their RM is usually the best person to provide the kind of detailed, on-the-job training that familiarizes them with the work and how to do it. One of the most common examples is that of walking new employees through the job and then observing them while they do it themselves.

Effective RMs should also be familiar with setting up off-site or off-the-job training for new hires, if for some reason they can't walk new employees through the job on-site. Off-site can take a number of different forms. For lower-level employees who are operating machinery or equipment, managers often use so-called vestibule training, which takes place in an environment that simulates the actual workplace. Once done with the vestibule training, new hires can be placed in an actual work setting where, with some coaching and support from their effective, experienced co-workers and direct reports, they can perform the job properly.

Some organizations use standard training and development programs for all of their personnel, while others tailor the training and development to the needs of the individual. For example, organizations often hire outside trainers and consultants for management or employee development in areas like computer programming, communication, and HR. Other companies give their RMs wide latitude to craft the most effective training. In this case, effective RMs identify the types of training and development that their people need and then provide the necessary programs. In large organizations, this may be coordinated under the auspices of the HR department, but effective RMs take it upon themselves if necessary; in small organizations RMs handle the arrangements on a department-by-department basis. One manager explained:

> *I have a budget for providing training to my people, and it's up to me to decide how this will be done. I have to handle everything. Usually I get outside trainers to handle the human relations material because I don't think we have anyone in-house who can do this training effectively. However, for on-the-job training to learn the job initially and work more efficiently, I do a lot of that myself. By walking around, seeing who has a problem mastering the technical side of their job, I have a pretty good idea of what is needed. Then I help them do it or I assign someone who can help.*

This RM's obvious ability and attentiveness to individual training needs allows him to craft training sequences that are efficient and effective. Of course, this relies on the RM being effective; poor managers, given such wide latitude, will train people poorly. Thus, we see the interconnectedness of all the management activities.

Regardless of the specific form, all of these training formats—in-house or outside consultants/firms, line employee or management training—have the same objective: to provide the participants with education and development that they can take back to the job and use to enhance their effectiveness and benefit the organization. Without this intermediate step of targeted training and follow-up for sustainability, employees will waste a great deal of time on ineffective work.

It should be evident that training exists on a spectrum from formal or one-size-fits-all events, workshops, or seminars, to informal, ad-hoc, individual training. The effective RM masters the whole spectrum, and is especially attentive to the kind of informal training, coaching, and counseling that they personally handle on a day-to-day basis. We usually call this mentoring and, more and more, coaching.

A mentor or coach counsels, teaches, and assists a specific individual or group. The semantic difference is instructive: Top-level executives, presumably effective already as they are, tend to get coaches; mentoring, on the other hand, is particularly important to young and/or new employees, and is therefore more closely associated with the HR activities of Real Managers. Most effective RMs make it a point to assign a mentor to each of their people and serve as one themselves. Mentors play an important role in identifying the training needs of their mentees, and thus help determine the effectiveness of their people's day-to-day work. One employee described such a nuts-and-bolts mentoring relationship in our study:

> The boss has been known to stop employees on the production line to demonstrate a correct procedure. He hasn't had any formal training for managing at this level, so he gets tips and suggestions and reads articles that Jack gives him. He's great at developing his subordinates. He sends clippings, makes telephone calls, gives tips, and often tells them about better ways to do things. He also tries to have his supervisory people attend as many motivational conferences and seminars as he can.

Mentors also show their people the ropes, explain how to use networks effectively, introduce their charges to people who can help their careers, and are available (i.e., have an open-door policy) should problems develop or advice be needed.

These relationships yield high returns. Those with a mentor are more likely to get ahead than their counterparts, a fact that the RMs in our study implied when they described their own mentors. Mentored employees also seem to be more satisfied with their career progress and the pleasure they derive from their work. The effect of this mentoring process is spelled out in the following example:

> *Mentoring is important to success. I go out of my way to provide it to my favorite young people coming up, even though we don't have a formal mentoring system. To me it's nothing more than a form of training and development, with a heavy sprinkling of realism. I try to tell those I'm mentoring the way it really is in this company. I want them to know the things to do and things not to do. For example, networking is important, but if you try to network with the wrong person, you may end up being tagged as "over-aggressive," and this can hurt your career. I try to teach my people how to avoid these problems. A lot of a young person's success in this company is knowing what to do and how to do it. A mentor can help ensure that the person he's helping out knows these things.*

Mentoring brings the full scope of human resource management into focus. Mentors take new employees, who have hopefully already been winnowed by a thoughtful and effective interview process, and teach them not only the rudiments of the actual job, but the intangible wisdom (implicit knowledge) of how to survive and get ahead in their specific organization.

Mentoring lies at the junction of effectiveness and success. As job training, mentoring is crucial for employees to master the elements of all kinds of jobs, from office and management tasks, to jobs in the new service economy, to traditional industrial work. Mentoring creates *effective* employees. But it also leads into another goal for effective

RMs; helping subordinates master their jobs so that they are ready to move on to other career opportunities. Career development is a natural outgrowth of mentoring, and it focuses on creating *successful* RMs. Some RMs in our study focused on this career development role:

> *One of the things I look for in a promotable person is competence. Does the individual know his job and does he do it well? If so, I think the person is ready to move up; if not, perhaps the individual has topped out, reached his level of incompetence, like in the Peter Principle.*

This RM shifted his focus from training his people in specific job roles—as an effective RM, he had taken care of that already—to emphasizing preparation for promotion, and evaluating his subordinates in terms of their readiness to move up.

Effective RMs help their employees build a resume or record that demonstrates their readiness to advance in their chosen career path: a "hero" file, as it were, in which they keep every reward, recommendation, performance evaluation, or memo related to their work output. Such documentation becomes important ammunition to support merit pay and promotion considerations. One manager explained:

> *Whenever one of my people does something particularly noteworthy, I make it a point to send this individual a memo. It doesn't necessarily go in the person's official personnel file, but I expect the individual to hang on to it. In this way, even if these people decide to leave the organization, this file can be used to support their job application. A hero file is important because sometimes you need to blow your own horn and be able to back it up with solid evidence.*

Providing documentation of their good work is part of how effective RMs assist subordinates with career development. More broadly, RMs help their subordinates identify career goals and formulate a plan for attaining these goals. In large organizations, the HR department is often an invaluable resource, supporting activities that contribute to the overall goal of career development; in medium and small organizations, effective RMs more often take this task upon themselves.

Career development needs a plan. Employees should begin by setting forth the goals they would like to attain during the next five or 10 years. The manager and the subordinate examine in concert how realistic these goals are both organizationally (is the career path in step with organizational practices?) and personally (does the individual have the ability to succeed?). Then they put together a plan to achieve these goals. The result is a short-range career plan that can be updated annually.

I try to help my people put together a career plan by focusing both on what they want to do and what the needs of the organization are likely to be over the next five to 10 years. If someone is a very successful salesperson and wants to move into the management ranks, obviously the individual will have to be promoted to local and then regional sales manager. The first areas of consideration are: What are the requirements to be promoted to a local sales manager's position?; How often are there openings at this level?; and How many people are currently in line? This gives us an idea of both where and how fast this salesperson can move. If the individual can expect to be promoted to this position within two years, and that is in line with her career plan, everything is fine. We will discuss the matter again when the promotion is at hand. If the person has little chance of getting the promotion or it will take longer than she wants to wait, we consider what other career moves are available to the individual and which of these is acceptable. We then begin discussing this new career path. You know, it's a lot of fun helping people work through their career plan. It makes me feel I am really helping them and I know it helps them get ahead.

This RM clearly spent an abundance of time with her employees, planning their short- and medium-term careers—and she made it a collaboration with each individual. But note as well her hint of the benefits that accrue to the RM, not least of which is her own job satisfaction. If performed effectively all the way through the process, human resource management can be a win for all sides instead of a necessary irritant.

Be that as it may, the sense of job satisfaction that stems from mentoring—"help[ing] them get ahead" doesn't necessarily translate to RM *success*. Our study showed that while human resource management activities are very important to *effective* RMs, ranking second behind communication in their relative relationship to RM effectiveness, they ranked last in the relative strength of relationship to RM success. In the comparative analysis, the top third of successful RMs did less of these activities than the bottom third.

This finding—that effective RMs give relative attention to human resource activities but successful RMs do not—has profound implications for today's organizations. For example, what does it say for those who believe in a human resource management approach, and its effectiveness, but want to get promoted? Pragmatically, our findings indicate that they could better spend their efforts on networking if they want to be promoted as quickly as possible. On the other hand, our data clearly show that those who take a human resource approach are more effective than those who give relatively more attention to networking.

The data lay bare a fundamental challenge for organizations, today and in the future. How can a 21st-century organization best align formal reward systems like promotion and pay raises with *effective* contributions of RMs? How can organizations cultivate managers who are effective **and** successful—at the same time? Ever since our original study revealed the strange dichotomy between success and effectiveness, this question has been, and continues to be, a central dilemma in management theory and especially management practice. We try to explore and find some answers in our concluding chapter.

CHAPTER **NINE**

The Real, Successful, Effective Manager in Today's Organizations

YOU, THE REAL MANAGER (OR FUTURE REAL MANAGER) are key to making your organization effective. But that's not your only goal; you also want to get ahead and move up in your own career, irrespective of the overall organization. These two goals—effectiveness and success—can work at cross-purposes. From the beginning of our study and this book, we wanted to answer three basic questions about individual RMs:

1. What do Real Managers do?
2. What do successful Real Managers do?
3. What do effective Real Managers do?

Figuring out some answers to these questions, and examining those answers in the context of the RM's day-to-day work life, also tells us how and why RMs are so central to the effectiveness of the overall organization: in other words, how individual effectiveness contributes to the purpose and goals of the overall organization. But personally, we wonder if you've been asking a fourth question:

4. What do Real Managers who are successful **and** effective do?

Many of the answers we've explored (prescriptions for ideal management, if you will) say that they will make you successful or effective—but not both. What can you, the RM in the middle of the daily grind, do to be both?

Let's start by reviewing our findings. Our study of Real Managers provided considerable data about their activities and in what relative proportions they do them. In particular, we found that Real Managers engage in traditional management activities (consisting of observable behaviors related to planning, decision-making, and controlling); routine communication activities (consisting of observable behaviors associated with exchanging routine information and handling paperwork); human resource management activities (consisting of observable behaviors descriptive of motivating/reinforcing, disciplining/punishing, managing conflict, staffing, and training/developing); and networking activities (consisting of observable behaviors associated with socializing/politicking and interacting with outsiders).

We introduced our study findings on all these activities in Chapter Two, and Figure 9-1 summarizes them. In brief, we found that RMs performed all four of the identified RM activities on a day-to-day basis relatively frequently. As shown, traditional management was 32% of the total, routine communication 29%, human resource management 20%, and networking 19%.

FIGURE 9-1
Relative Frequencies of Managerial Activities for all RMs (n=248)

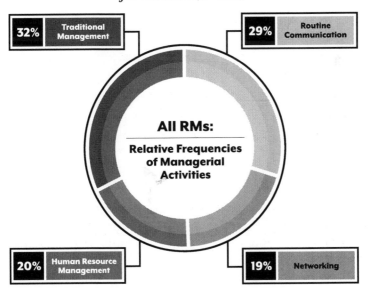

| 32% | Traditional Management |
| 29% | Routine Communication |

All RMs:

Relative Frequencies of Managerial Activities

| 20% | Human Resource Management |
| 19% | Networking |

It's not surprising that traditional management and routine communication activities take up the majority of RMs' time: 61%. These are, after all, the things most managers do in the conventional wisdom. But it's not an overwhelming majority; we should not discount the considerable emphasis RMs give to human resource management and networking. In particular, we should note that about one out of every five activities was networking, which is generally ignored in traditional management literature. We should also recognize that the explosion of social media networking in recent years has undoubtedly had profound effects on workplace relationships. The precise effects of electronic communication and social media on management is a tale yet to be told; it may be that its ubiquity in some ways encourages and intensifies certain RM activities like communication and networking, while atrophying other aspects of those activities.

We designed three different, and rigorous, ways to analyze RM activities (as detailed in Chapter Three), and all had a common and revealing finding: *successful managers network*. Let's review the numbers to drive home this crucial point. All three analyses showed that successful RMs give relatively different emphasis to certain managerial activities than do their unsuccessful counterparts. First and most important, we found through statistical analysis that successful RMs did significantly more networking. The other activities—traditional management, routine communication, and human resources—had no significant relationship to RM success. Drilling down a little further, our comparative descriptive analysis, in which we asked RMs descriptive questions about their work and compared the results from different groups of them, revealed that the top third of successful RMs were doing a great deal more networking and slightly more communicating activities than the bottom third. Importantly, in this comparative analysis, we found that the successful RMs were doing relatively less human resource and traditional management activities than the bottom third.

When we ranked the relative strengths of the managerial activities' relationship to RM success, we saw that, as with the other two analyses, the networking activity had the strongest relative relationship to RM success. Although human resource activities fared somewhat better and communication activities somewhat worse in this relative strength of relationship analysis than in the comparative analysis, all three analyses (statistical, comparative, and relative strength of relationship) found what many observers, both inside and out of the management scene, have suspected for years; the way to get ahead and be successful in organizations is to give a lot of attention to networking (that is, socializing/politicking and interacting with outsiders).

So much for success; to get ahead, network. But what about *effective* managers? They are, after all, among the most crucial cogs in the management machine and much more important to attaining organizational purpose and goals than managers who know how to get promoted. The effectiveness question has traditionally been the most important one, both to management theorists and real-life organizations. It's also the most difficult to answer. Our study results reported in Chapter Four indicated that communication activities were the most strongly related to managerial effectiveness, followed, in turn, by human resource and traditional management activities. The most interesting finding was that networking had the weakest relationship to managerial effectiveness. This, of course, is in stark contrast to the success analysis result: basically, the very activity that most strongly led to success for RMs did relatively little to make them effective managers. Conversely, communication and human resource management activities had the strongest relationships to effective Real Managers in our comprehensive study.

The study data lead to an inescapable conclusion: Successful managers are not the same people as effective managers. All managers basically perform the same day-to-day activities, ones familiar both to readers of management literature and to managers on the ground—to whit, traditional management, communication, human resources, and networking. But the successful RMs are not necessarily doing the same activities as the effective ones. Can this be true? And what about that rarest of species: the RM who is both successful *and* effective?

SUCCESSFUL/EFFECTIVE MANAGERS

Some managers have it all. They get promoted quickly, and at the same time, they manage effectively; they have satisfied and committed subordinates and run high-performing units. We have made a clear distinction throughout the book between these management activities and approaches, but some RMs seem to manage both. However, since successful and effective RMs exhibited such different sets of activities, we did not expect to find many examples of this endangered species. Sure enough, there were very few. But, in our view, this makes it even more important to understand them.

Thus, the last phase of our analysis studied those relatively few RMs who are both successful *and* effective. Our large, heterogeneous sample of 178 RMs gave us enough data to calculate the success index defined in Chapter Three and the effectiveness index defined in Chapter Four. Because we used only the top third of each sample in our previous analyses, we applied the same rule here. Thus, in order to determine those RMs that were both successful and effective, we took the top third of successful RMs and the top third of effective RMs and identified those that were common to both groups. As shown in Figure 9-2, we found 15 RMs who were both successful and effective according to this procedure.

FIGURE 9-2
Determination of Successful and Effective RMs (n=15)

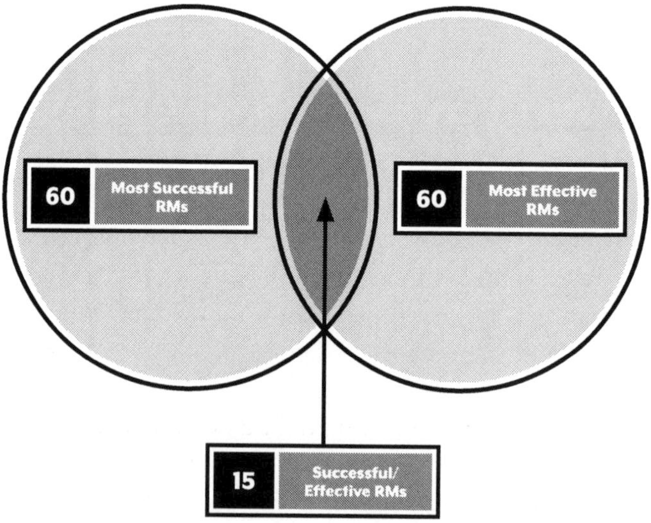

Remember, from our previous analyses on successful and effective RMs, we found that successful RMs are not generally the same as effective RMs: the former do more networking while the latter concentrate on communication and human resources. However, for the few cases where RMs are both successful *and* effective (including those 15 out of a sample of 178), *their activities are almost identical to RMs as a whole.* To put it another way, RMs who are successful and effective do not seem to do the activities of either successful or effective RMs alone or some unique hybrid of the two. Instead, successful *and* effective RMs portion their activities in ways that are very similar to RMs in general.

Figure 9-3 shows the breakdown of each of the major activities for the 15 successful *and* effective RMs. The relative frequencies are almost identical to those from all 248 RMs we observed in the study (see Figure 2-3). This was also true of the sample of 178 RMs we used in the present analysis.

FIGURE 9-3
Relative Frequencies of Managerial Activities
for Successful and Effective RMs (n=15)

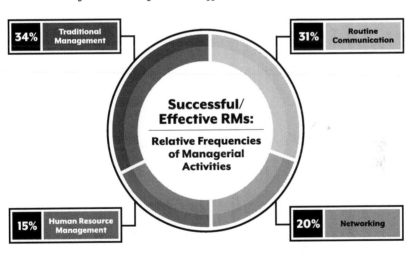

We should be careful reaching definitive conclusions concerning successful/effective RMs because of the small number of RMs that met the criteria. But why are there so few? This is a more interesting question, with potentially greater implications for today's organizations, especially when combined with our key finding that successful managers are *not* the same as effective managers. To put it succinctly: successful managers concentrate mostly on one thing, effective managers concentrate on completely different things, and rarely do the twain meet. These strange and seemingly counterintuitive conclusions have far-reaching implications for the present and future performance of our organizations—particularly for any organization that can figure out how to cultivate those superstar successful/effective RMs.

What does all this mean for today's RMs in the trenches? Well, if you can figure out how to be both successful and effective, you will be in a truly select group of the best RMs. Here's the good news: there is no secret formula to it, nor do you need to reinvent the management wheel. In other words, those few RMs in our study that are both successful and effective are not really distinctive from Real Managers in general in terms of the things they do day-to-day (although presumably they are also quite good at all those things). They use a balanced approach to their activities. This, in and of itself, is revealing. It says that in order to be successful *and* effective, no management activity can be ignored. In the last analysis, our study verified empirically the importance of all of the traditional management, communication, networking, and human resource management activities we described in previous chapters. Perhaps best of all, these conclusions jibe with all of our instincts about management in the actual workplace. Good managers are jacks-of-all-trades. Bad managers either get fired, or (the worst) are so good at sucking up to the big boss that they get promoted before their incompetence catches up to them. The best managers have a good relationship with the ultimate boss, get along with and are trusted by their individual subordinates, team, peers, and upper management, and know how to get stuff done.

REAL MANAGERS AND MODERN MANAGEMENT THINKING

A host of popular books aimed at practicing managers has flooded the market in the past few decades (we call these "airport books"). While a lot of fluff has accompanied the lasting work, together all these books comprise popular management thinking. For the most part, though, these books are nothing more (or less) than enjoyable, journalistic descriptions. Does our comprehensive (quantitative and qualitative) research back them up? How do the four scientifically derived RM activities correspond to modern management thinking? We have reviewed many of these books and found that the traditional management, human resource management, routine communication, and networking activities not only generally fit well, but can also be useful as a common base—a way to interpret other currently popular approaches to effective management.

One of these approaches is called "transformational management." It derives from the work of Bernard Bass, Bruce Avolio and other organizational leadership scholars, who have argued that performance-based reward systems are old fashioned. It has also percolated into many of those airport books we just mentioned. In traditional, transactional, performance-based systems, the manager identifies or even creates subordinates' needs, and arranges rewards (or consequences) to satisfy those needs in exchange for work-related performance. In the new transformational management, on the other hand, the manager tries to get subordinates believing in superordinate goals (that is, goals that are larger or in some way more profound than personal goals or day-to-day targets) and such higher-order needs as Abraham Maslow's classic self-actualization and Avolio's authentic (genuine, ethical) self-leadership. Transformational management does not rely on traditional reward systems, but on charismatic and inspirational leadership. For example, in practice, subordinates might be inspired to believe that they are at the cutting edge of a great organizational change for the better, that they are the greatest or best or most capable employees in the world, and that the changes will help them reach their full potential as contributing members of a better society.

Those are lofty goals indeed! To make this transformational approach happen in real work settings, the RM has to be able to sensitize their people to the importance of the superordinate goals, demonstrate that the goals are in fact achievable, and provide credibility. For the transformational approach to be successful, the RM has to convince subordinates, peers, and even superiors to get behind such high-minded, abstruse goals; therefore, it hinges on the manager's skill as a leader and communicator. A skilled communicator and human resource manager under the transformational approach can provide positive reinforcement and confidence and can deliberately alter organizational culture in a positive way. One can readily find examples of transformational management in the Oracle of Omaha, Warren Buffet, the serial entrepreneur, Elon Musk, or Microsoft's Bill Gates. Some of these figures have become legendary icons in popular culture; think of the cult of personality that still surrounds Apple's Steve Jobs, a self-identified transformational manager if there ever was one, years after his death.

Transformational management fits in perfectly—indeed, it confirms—the significance of our research. Transformational managers, in an ideal sense, are the ultimate effective RMs. Recall that communication and human resource management are the two major contributing activities to RM effectiveness. Since these two traits represent the two key elements in transformational management as well, this means that RMs who are effective by our measurements are ideally situated to be transformational leaders. We can also speculate that engaging in transformational leadership is a good way to spur the RMs to *success* as well, thus putting them on the road to entering that rarest of categories, successful/effective RMs.

The elements of transformational leadership might sound to you like an opaque way of saying "motivational"; just another kind of rah-rah boosterism. Indeed, another school of thought casts a suspicious eye on motivation; Samuel Culbert and John McDonough cite it as one of the most misused concepts in management in their "radical management" approach. They claim that in its perverted form, motivation is defined as: (1) getting someone to want what the manager wants; (2) arranging reward/punishment consequences to produce performance demanded by the manager; and (3) forcing poor workers or people with grievances to perform when the manager has no knowledge of the reasons for their bad behavior. Radical management is instead centered on trust. Trust, by this way of thinking, is motivating, and organizations that achieve high levels of trust among their members are likely to be the most successful.

This trust-based approach may seem like altruism, but it's not—not really. At one level, we can think of it as confidence in the elements of effective management; if you're an effective RM, you should expect your team to be effective even if you're not constantly dangling evanescent rewards (monetary or psychological) in front of them. Viewed from another direction, it's just common sense. After all, if you ask yourself the question, "Have you ever bought anything from, or had very much to do with, someone you didn't trust?", what would your answer be?

At the risk of oversimplifying, radical management is implemented on three levels. At the first level, counseling, managers develop an accommodation between a single organization member's personal needs and the organization's needs. They also work to convince others in the environment to recognize that the niche the person has chosen to fill contributes significantly to the organization. (Managers are actually engaging in a constructive advising/counseling/negotiating process in this stage.) To do their part effectively, managers must be secure enough to remain unthreatened by their subordinates' selected goals, and by the means they select to achieve those goals. Here, again, effective communication and human resource management becomes essential. However, networking, the hallmark of the successful RM, can also be helpful if the subordinate is to be included in one of the manager's networks.

Team building constitutes the second implementation level of radical management. Effective team building convinces employees to recognize the value of their coworkers' jobs: in effect, that the niches others have chosen to fill also contribute significantly to the organization. Here, RMs can draw on their skill as a peacemaker in managing conflict; team building is a natural outcome of that particular human resource management activity. Just as subordinate members of the work unit are developing interpersonal tolerance and understanding, the RM is working her human resources muscle. In other words, this second level of radical management is a perfect fit with effective management as we define it.

The third level of radical management, brokering, addresses two objectives. First, it advocates for the work unit or group as a distinctive entity among other work units (for example, to get other work units to value the positive contribution of the manager's work unit). Second, it develops the most productive correspondence between the niches subordinates select to fill (what different work units are doing) and the expectations of the client environment (the larger organization). In other words, brokering gets everyone in the work unit to adjust their roles in order to get to a point where they are, in the words of Nobel Laureate Herbert Simon's classic concept, "satisficing" the expectations of their manager's boss or outside clients; in other words, they are not necessarily perfect, not necessarily maximizing every bit of their talent and time, but are performing well enough. Brokering allows them to adjust the expectations of upper management or outside clients to fit whatever the work unit does best. This part of the radical management process brings all of the RM's activities into play; it requires effective communication, human resource management, traditional management, and networking.

It should be obvious in this radical management approach that managers need to be secure in their position and able to act maturely with their subordinates. If they feel threatened by their subordinates' contributions, they will not be able to implement the approach successfully. For example, a competitive or subservient leader/subordinate relationship precludes trust and renders the full potential of the approach unattainable. RMs who believe that their subordinates are inferior to themselves are simply not ready to implement the third step—they aren't ready to "sell" their work unit.

To reiterate, the radical management approach fits with our four empirically derived RM activities, and also with our findings about RM success and effectiveness. But it's not necessarily a way to achieve the success/effectiveness holy grail. Effective RMs, it appears, implement the counseling and team-building steps (that is, communication and human resource management activities), while successful RMs emphasize the brokering and team-building steps (that is, networking activities). In other words, radical management fits well with successful and effective RMs, but it doesn't necessarily create both at the same time.

Both transformational and radical management require RMs to hone their skills at providing feedback. The idea of giving objective performance feedback, which, as we have seen, motivates employees and enhances their job satisfaction, is, surprisingly, relatively new in management theory. Feedback provides valued information, recognition, and attention for employees. Applied to goal setting, RMs use feedback to correct deviations from a goal or from the manager's performance expectations. High achievers need immediate feedback as well; it's a key motivator and reinforces effective work. But whether motivational or corrective, the act of feedback is important in and of itself, at least with today's human resources. In many cultures, ostracism is used as formal punishment; the manager simply ignores and shunts aside the misbehaving employee. In modern organizations, we do not formally build in such punishment, but by not providing personal, objective feedback to employees, we create a similar situation.

It may feel to some RMs that their group is too big for them to be constantly providing feedback, or that they just don't have enough time in the day. Make time! Lack of feedback can have serious consequences. Managers can build feedback into the job design so that their employees know immediately how they are doing. For example, semi-automated test equipment in critical assembly-line alignment or adjustment processes, and of course the process of face-to-face sales, can give real-time feedback. But regardless of feedback from the job itself, employees can and should get feedback from their supervisors. Just as employees dislike manipulation, they chafe at having their existence ignored.

We found that successful RMs use feedback liberally in their networking activities, to pay their debts, furnish information, and reinforce the behavior of other members of the network for supporting them. If they fail to do this they are likely to be expelled from their respective networks. At the same time, effective RMs provide feedback in the course of their communication and human resource activities with subordinates. Whether they are getting ahead or getting the job done and satisfying subordinates, RMs know that positive feedback provides positive results. They also know that negative feedback, given in anger, contempt, or with the hope that the subordinate or peer who receives it will fail, is difficult to disguise and only humiliates and alienates. As we described earlier, effective managers follow what we called PIGS (positive, immediate, graphic, and specific) performance feedback.

ORGANIZATIONAL FRAMEWORKS, OLD AND NEW

We often ask ourselves how serious workplace misunderstandings and high levels of conflict or unresponsiveness can happen when "everyone knows" the importance of the task at hand. The problem is (perhaps), everyone *doesn't* know it. A recent way of thinking about organizations, worked out by scholars Lee Bolman and Terrence Deal, described four perspectives, or frameworks, about organizations. It's a kind of safari through the organizational theory jungle, and one that purports to arrive at that point of near-perfect information—the point where "everyone knows." Bolman and Deal's frameworks are:

1. *The rational systems perspective*, which focuses on the fit between the organizations' goals, roles, technology, purpose, structure, and environment.

2. *The human resource perspective*, which focuses on relationships between the organization and its people; their needs, skills, and culture; and the mechanisms for maximizing mutual benefit.

3. *The political perspective*, which emphasizes how organizational actors obtain or control scarce resources, influence, power, conflict, and conflict resolution.

4. *The symbolic perspective*, which emphasizes how stories, legends, symbols, rituals, and ceremonies give meaning to the organization.

Bolman and Deal claim that each of these four frameworks can contribute in fundamental and powerful ways to an organization, and that organizations are most effective when the four perspectives are balanced with each other—when they are "aligned." The four perspectives also correspond to specific management functions and concerns. For example, the rational systems perspective, which they call the "structural frame," outlines how organizations provide direction for their goals, define their various internal structures, and go about getting things done ("task accomplishment," as Bolman and Deal call it). The human resource perspective addresses the use of human resources sensitivity to impact human needs effectively. The political perspective encompasses resource allocation, conflict, and strategies to obtain power. Finally, the symbolic perspective concentrates on shaping a cohesive organizational culture of shared values, symbols, and practices.

When groups and individuals in a single organization are exclusively focused on different frameworks, it is virtually impossible for them to communicate. For example, an organization member with a human resource-based perspective (such as a participative management approach) would be regarded with suspicion or contempt by an organization member with a purely politically oriented perspective. The political operator would believe that power is the major factor in her subordinates' performance, while human resource activity is important only to the extent that it controls confrontation and conflict—or if it leads to more power. To her counterpart who sees things from a human resources perspective, the political orientation is immorally manipulative and disregards the concept that employees want to do the right thing, in as autonomous an environment as possible. So, these clashing perspectives—one hierarchical, with clear lines of power and control, the other more nimble or flexible and allowing self-directed work—have the potential to open up a Pandora's box of poor communication and a toxic organizational culture.

Cultural memory can also block organizations from aligning their frameworks. For example, suppose a union is taking a firm stand in current labor negotiations, and the history of labor relations in the organization (to the labor side) is replete with activist union heroes and management villains. The labor side accepts an adversarial relationship between management and labor as fact, or even received wisdom. Not to be outdone, management has equally adversarial stories to tell about the union. These contrasting stories comprise the organization's cultural memory, and they can be very influential, not to mention frustrating to union or management negotiators who are seeking explanations and solutions in a rational systems frame of reference, not a cultural framework. Clearly, establishing a common ground for negotiation in the face of such mutually inflammatory perspectives is a difficult task, one that negotiators can't achieve without a keen perception of the underlying perspectives and the real issues.

These organizational frameworks fit well with our four categories of RM activities. RMs' traditional management and communication activities largely cover the rational systems perspective. The human resource perspective directly translates to RM human resource activities, while the political perspective corresponds to RM networking activities. Thus, directly observable RM activities correlate with the rational systems, human resource, and political perspectives of organization. By definition, however, the symbolic perspective does not correspond with any directly observable RM activities. We will examine cultural symbols and practices as they pertain to organizations at the end of the chapter.

Although the RM activities seem to fit well with the state-of-the-art and non-traditional management ideas discussed so far, what about more conventional approaches to management practice? Most of the conventional literature focuses on common concerns shared by all employees. For example, pretty much all employees want to know why they are participating in their organizations. "Why do I work here?" they ask; "What makes it distinctively different from being elsewhere?" The organization should have a fully developed philosophy, but after its leaders have stated that philosophy, the organization has to put it into practice—they have to walk the talk. Maintaining the organization's credibility by adhering to an overall philosophy becomes a full-time job. When that credibility begins to wane, employees start to worry, and this is reflected in their commitment to the organization. You, as an effective RM not much concerned with philosophy, can employ day-to-day communication and human resource management activities to help your employees get past their concerns.

Of course, employees are always concerned with what is expected of them, and clear expectations often run aground on the shoals of conflicting goals. New employees tend to prefer clear goals to uncertain or complex ones, but older employees (including many managers) have gained the experience and sensitivity to become more observant and are outraged when their organization's stated goals and actual managerial behavior appear to be incongruent or contradictory. Having been in the trenches, they feel betrayed by too-clear, too-perfect, and ultimately unrealistic goals. There are at least six types of organizational goals:

1. *Stated goals*: the announced goals of the organization or management, which serve as performance targets for employees.
2. *Stereotypical goals*: the goals commonly regarded as socially acceptable and reputable.
3. *Existing goals*: the combined goals of the organization's members that are part of the organizational culture.
4. *Honorific goals*: the goals that impute admirable qualities to the organization—"boy scout" goals.
5. *Taboo goals*: real but covert organizational goals.

6. Repressed goals: real goals, pursued actively, if sometimes unconsciously, that contradict the organization's self-image and values.

All of these types are potentially contradictory: just think, for example, of a big corporation announcing high-flown customer-care goals while cutting service staff. There are innumerable examples, all of which can create roadblocks and frustrations for employees trying to align their work with a perceived maze of conflicting goals. If organizational participants seek truth in this mixture of goals, they can usually find double-speak in several flavors. For the effective RM, all this points directly to the importance of human resource management.

Given the common uncertainty with conflicting goals, employees are also concerned with how they're doing; in other words, they need feedback and advice. They want to know how their activities will benefit them, and who will provide what kinds of help when they need it. To respond to these specific concerns, RMs utilize communication and human resource management activities, which, unlike traditional management activities, convey the personal interest and credibility of the manager. Basically, RMs know that communicating effectively and keeping the human resource management machine well-oiled are the best ways to alleviate these employee concerns and get their activity properly aligned with organizational goals. It's not surprising, therefore, that the effective RMs in our study emphasized communication and human resource management activities over traditional management activities.

In fact, the key concepts and courses of action that most conventional management theory recommends for practitioners maps pretty closely to the activities that Real Managers focus on day to day. In Table 9-1, we have marked which of the four RM activities we believe are most essential to accomplish each of these conventional concepts or courses of action effectively.

TABLE 9-1
Concepts and Courses of Action Recommended in the Conventional Literature, Fit to RM Activities

CONCEPT/ COURSE OF ACTION	HUMAN RESOURCE MANAGEMENT	ROUTINE COMMUNICATION	NETWORKING	TRADITIONAL MANAGEMENT
	RELEVANT RM ACTIVITIES			
Adding value	X	X		X
Addressing real underlying issues	X	X	X	X
Charismatic leadership	X		X	
Consequence analysis				X
Defusing tension	X	X	X	
Developing, promotability among subordinates	X		X	
Managing by motivation	X			
Effective teams	X			
Expressing expectations	X	X		X
Feedback	X	X		
Legitimizing leadership ability and credibility	X			X
Listening skills	X	X		
Matching employee personal and professional goals	X	X		
Not routinizing to death	X		X	
Performance-based reward	X			X
Quality circles	X	X		
Reinforcing interdependence	X		X	
Specifying productive work behaviors	X	X		X
Transforming intentions into results	X	X		X
Trust-based management	X	X	X	
Using lateral relationships	X	X	X	

Interestingly, we find that our estimate of essential RM activities appears across the sample list of conventional concepts and courses of action in the same relative order and frequency as our empirical findings for their relative contribution to RM effectiveness (in order: communication, human resource management, traditional management, and networking). Whether the managerial framework is traditional or relatively new, it's abundantly clear that effective managers need to do a great deal of communication and human resource management activities—which is precisely what our evidence indicates that effective RMs are doing. Meanwhile, less effective managers, who are more tightly focused on traditional planning, decision-making, and controlling activities, as well as socializing/politicking and interacting with outsider activities, are not utilizing the full potential of their human resources.

In recent years, some management thinkers and business leaders have justified a narrow traditional management focus, no matter its problems or other options available to the modern organization, simply because it supposedly maximizes productivity. Ironically, because of all the human factors we have detailed, that formula turns out to be inadequate. What we now call "traditional" management practice was, a century ago, an evolutionary step prompted by economic necessity; it fulfilled a need for greater efficiency and less waste of resources. Now, however, managers in many competing nations have a clearer understanding than we seem to in the United States that people are also resources, and that they can make greater differences in productivity than can refinements in planning, decision-making, and controlling (the traditional management activities).

For example, in the 1980s and 1990s the Japanese gave top priority to a formal strategy of human resource management. They implemented human resource techniques such as participative management (for example, quality circles) and overall human resource policies (for example, lifetime employment) while most American organizations are still just talking about them. Today, we are once again prompted by economic necessity to greater efficiency and fewer wasted resources. We can't afford to waste human resource potential, and the most effective RMs are taking it upon themselves to maximize these activities.

MANAGEMENT SKILLS FOR THE PRESENT AND FUTURE

As a Real Manager, you can aim for success (getting promoted) or effectiveness (being the best manager around, by whatever measurables your organization uses)—or even both, as we have seen. Regardless of your choice, our research shows that the most successful RMs and the most keenly effective RMs do things differently than their less successful and effective counterparts. The good news is that these activities are all trainable skills. Let's try to equate RM activities to current training and development needs, and project some implications for these skills into the future.

Effective managers are effective communicators. But they have to know more than how to write and verbalize understandable instructions. They also need to understand the effects of what they write and say, including the implications of writing or saying too much or too little. For example, a written warning to a subordinate documenting his or her poor performance and a circulated memo that formalizes a specific objective may be necessary and proper activities. The question is, how do your employees receive these written communications? Effective communication is two-sided.

Writing just to establish a paper trail—the CYA syndrome—devastates trust; so does the infamous "poisonous memo" used to document a biased, one-sided interpretation or position. In fact, you should consider using written communication sparingly to begin with. If you're sensitive to the effects of formal written memos, you'll realize that there are few things potentially more uninspiring, or even more hateful, than a poorly written or thoughtlessly conceived memo, email, or text. Managers who put too much information in writing eventually dull the ear of the receiver. Organization members eventually disregard nagging communicators, regardless of their rank.

It's equally important to listen; messages, whether verbal or written, are not always what they appear to be. Listening is a highly individualistic skill, and unfortunately an individual manager's leadership style is not necessarily a good indicator of his or her listening skill. Autocratic managers might be expected to be poor listeners because they believe that their subordinates should simply follow their orders. More human-oriented managers might be expected to be more empathetic listeners. Indeed, the traditional management literature tends to denigrate the autocratic management style. Yet the autocratic manager may be a sensitive, perceptive listener, regardless of the hierarchical obedience they seem to expect. Similarly, human resources-oriented managers may in fact be insensitive and unresponsive listeners. Good communication skills don't necessarily correspond to good human resources skills.

For example, it's common for RMs to issue standing invitations—an open door—to their subordinates to visit and discuss problems. One such manager in our study listened to a valid grievance for two hours, took copious notes, and then did nothing to change the situation. The subordinate was more dissatisfied after the interaction than before. The RM's listening objective was to let the subordinate vent his feelings and to gather as much information about the subordinate as possible. Their duplicity ensured that any semblance of two-way communication was lacking from the beginning. To be clear: the manager didn't interrupt; he was courteous to the subordinate; he gave all of the return cues to indicate that he was paying attention. Was he a skillful listener? Evidently not.

RMs who are passive, insensitive, or unresponsive may be good listeners, in the sense of taking in information, but they lack the ability to translate information and intentions into effective action. They simply adjust their listening behavior to the management style that suits them—the one they're used to. In contrast, RMs who do translate information and intentions into action are open to changing their management style based on what they learned by listening. The point is that being a good listener does not guarantee being an effective manager. However, being a poor listener virtually guarantees being an ineffective manager, because managers who are poor listeners simply have less information with which to work.

The RM who is a skillful listener can also hear more deeply hidden messages. These might be in the background and have little to do with whatever present work issue you're discussing, but they can be invaluable, both for the RM who is trying to understand his employees and the employee trying to fit in and get ahead. These messages might be generalized concerns or observations about their work environment: What does the sender of the message see as the real issues that affect them?; Why do employees sometimes fantasize achievements that they haven't accomplished (that is, confuse their intent to do things with actually doing them)?; Why does someone maintain a high or low profile, or constantly name-drop?; How do they feel about the organization's culture, organizational changes, or good and bad things happening to the organization? Or they might be messages about someone's attitudes or life experience that constitute useful knowledge for future work-related issues, concerns, or successes: What is someone's self-image?; What is their sense of time?; What are their aspirations or priorities?; How is their home life, and does it complement or conflict with their work?

Being sensitive to these background hints helps you, the RM, make accommodations to better suit the employee to the job, or draw restrictions that circumscribe potential bad behavior. It takes practice and time, but the alternative is more uncertainty and risk. Effective RMs have these communication skills. Similarly, RMs working at their networking and human resource management activities need to work on skills that help them develop and maintain productive interpersonal relationships. No loner was ever good at networking.

Our analysis points out the importance of focusing on interpersonal skills: RMs in our study who concentrated on traditional management activities, largely to the exclusion of the other three activity areas, were both less effective and less successful. Sometimes managers get fixated on traditional methods out of habit, but it's more likely they're avoiding activities that demand interpersonal skills. Talking to people is hard, after all! It can be draining, and requires quick thinking and improvisation. Traditional management activities (particularly where quantitative planning, decision-making, and controlling methods can be applied) are often more certain and less messy than the other human resource management, communication, and networking activities—the ones that require interpersonal skills.

Managers with a low tolerance for ambiguity tend to concentrate on such traditional activities; they can often be accomplished in private as well, where no one can see the manager struggle. The other RM activities are more spontaneous, and always involve an audience (bosses, subordinates, peers, or outsiders) to witness one's mistakes. The word says it all—interpersonal skills involve *inter*action with *persons*. It may seem to be the most obvious thing in the world, but it is surprising how many managers, most of whom probably think they have great interpersonal skills, believe they can do their job without ever running into another person. Effective managers need to practice interacting with their peers, subordinates, and superiors.

Nearly all Real Managers live in sometimes-stressful environments. In the normal course of doing their jobs, they experience high levels of ambiguity and often try to change organizations and people resistant to change. Stress and frustration, from a multitude of annoyances and situations large and small, pervades modern organizational life. For a manager, it might be the stress of responsibility for the performance or the welfare of others. For employees, it can be their lack of involvement in decisions that affect them directly; or it might be fear of the performance evaluation. The work environment itself is stressful: it can be crowded, noisy, uncomfortably hot or cold—bad working conditions unfortunately are still a source of stress for many of today's employees. Finally, organizational change, necessary as it often is, feeds and intensifies stress.

These stressors are not all automatically bad, but all of them have the potential to adversely affect physical and mental health as well as work performance. Peoples' perceptions of the cause of stress, and the social support they receive to combat it, determine how resistant they are to it. Support from the organization is key: For example, an employee in poor health (a major cause of stress) perceives his company's health policies or insurance as a welcome aid in stressful times—or perhaps as a hindrance.

As a Real Manager, you play a central role in helping your subordinates manage stress. Socializing employees effectively, communicating with them, and supporting them in many other ways (all activities of the effective RM) all alleviate stress. For example, giving your direct reports wide latitude to make decisions that directly affect them can reduce their stress. So can adjusting reward systems to be fair and performance-based. In general, RMs who want to create a less stressful work environment will encourage both upward and downward communication.

Change is inherently stressful, even when it's necessary. RMs must be able to successfully introduce and manage change. Planning change and preparing, intervening, and restructuring work and the organization are only part of the change process. As in athletics, music, and romance, timing is everything; knowing when to act is also a key part of the management process during times of change. Under the most favorable conditions, change requires traditional management activities: planning, deciding, and controlling. Effective management of change also requires communication and human resource management activities, to minimize the threat of change and prepare others to accept and support the change. RM networking can also be an invaluable resource during change, to provide supplemental resources, to fill in the gaps, when they are needed.

These RM activities overlap and reinforce each other as organizations evolve. For example, when change removes an essential routine like a communication channel, it has to be replaced with an equally or more effective one that satisfies both organizational and individual needs and desires. Controlling this is a function of traditional management. However, a complex combination of networking, communication, and human resource management activities lies behind resolving the consequent interpersonal problems among peers or subordinates during the implementation phase. These overlapping requirements point to the need for hybrid managers with a range of eclectic skills; most of all, managers who can work with people effectively (as we hope is clear by now).

What does all this mean for the future? What new management skills will tomorrow's workplace demand for success and effectiveness? Surprisingly, our research suggests to us that no revolutionary new skills will be needed in the near future. Instead, we anticipate that the demands on the skills we've discussed above will intensify. In the global marketplace, the demand for effective RMs, and the opportunities open to successful ones, will only continue to increase. Emerging nations, especially in East Asia, have been quick to adopt human resource management techniques that have been heretofore largely ignored in the West, but worker demands and expectations have lagged far behind that adoption. High technology has become easily exportable for production by minimally skilled workers overseas. Emerging nations will continue to follow this pattern. The net result will be that our present problems with labor costs will also intensify over the near future, as new nations join the labor market. But in the ever-increasing jostle of global competition, there will always be a market for the human factor, and for RMs who know how to attain, develop, and lead it.

A major part of this global equation lies in our cultural values concerning productivity and competence. How much should employees produce, how knowledgeable should they be about their jobs, and how receptive should they be to retraining? Changing perceptions and expectations will require changes both in organizational and general societal values. To be effective in this environment, RMs will need to have a broad base of knowledge and skills on which to draw. They will have to view situations from many perspectives and be sensitive to the effects of their own behavior. They will need to be courageous enough to test themselves and to retain their optimism. We think that RMs will respond well to these challenges.

CLOSURE AND A POINT OF DEPARTURE:
Will the Real RM Please Stand Up?

The idea of corporate or organizational culture made the leap from scholarly concern to popular buzzword a long time ago, to the point where we have seen at least one senior-level manager order his corporate staff to "create a corporate culture by next week." But what exactly is a corporate culture, and why does it matter to the RM?

An organizational culture consists of the shared understandings, norms, values, attitudes, and beliefs within an organization. It has also been expressed as the organization's basic values, philosophy, and financial, technical, and human concerns. It is reflected in the organization's stories, humor, role models, symbols, ceremonies, concepts of time, beliefs about human nature, responsiveness to the external environment, and performance expectations for its employees. When new employees are taken into the organization, they undergo a socialization process in which they learn the values, beliefs, and behaviors that are expected of them. One outcome of this process is that organizational members develop shared interpretations of work-related events.

In short, an organizational culture is very much like an organizational "personality," and like a human personality, it is a complex amalgam comprised of a constellation of traits, gathered over a long developmental period. Many of these cultural traits of organizations are useful and necessary. Some are not. For example, on the positive side, making high-risk, high-value decisions cautiously is normally both useful and necessary. However, when the organization carries that caution to excess—when it ceases to respond to its competitive environment—the element of caution in the organizational culture becomes a drag on success. Expectations of infallibility in a corporate culture often include severe penalties for failure, which extinguish risk-taking and initiative.

Effective management demands that RMs recognize which characteristics of the organization's culture are useful and which must be changed so that the organization can remain or become effective. As with human personality, unless the organization recognizes and accepts its need to change, those seeking to alter the organizational personality or culture do so at their own peril. We talked earlier about the inherent stress of change; the process of shaping organizational culture is a part of change, and RMs must handle it gradually and with care.

Can managers really shape their organizational cultures? As the social tapestry outside the organization changes and new generations of employees join the organization, their expectations regarding working conditions, wages and salaries, and performance-related rewards differ from those of earlier generations, often resulting in conflict. This levies a requirement for managers to develop an accommodation between the organizational and the new social culture in the same way that they develop an accommodation between existing physical facilities and procedures with new technology. In effect, organizational culture is always gradually changing.

Let's see how the four RM activities fit with such an analysis of organizational culture. How can a manager shape organizational culture to establish a success-oriented, rather than mediocre or failure-oriented, environment? RMs intending to do this must alter the organization's basic values, its philosophy, and its financial, technical, and human concerns. This starts at a fundamental human level: changing shared understandings, norms, values, attitudes, and beliefs within their organization. RMs translate these cultural intentions into action by adding to or replacing the organization's stories, humor, role models, symbols, ceremonies, concepts of time, beliefs about human nature, responsiveness to the external environment, or performance expectations for employees.

Does this sound complicated, or impossible? The fact is that you, as an RM, are doing this all the time. You constantly change these cultural mores, symbols, and practices through your day-to-day work—it's just that you are probably unaware of its effect on organizational culture. Your successes and failures, as well as those of your peers, bosses, and subordinates, narrate organizational stories. When you tell your peers at the bar after work about that hair-raising sales call, that improvisation that saved your bacon in meeting the monthly production goal, or the speech to a convention session that you hilariously flubbed, you are, bit by bit, changing organizational culture. And when you convey your values and expectations through your activities (communication, human resource management, traditional management, and networking), you alter shared norms, values, attitudes, beliefs, and understandings. Even your *in*activity has such effects. Each time you do something, refrain from doing something, or behave in a different way, you either reinforce the status quo or add a little weight to the beginning of future change.

Simply stated, the real organization is always in a state of flux or change. How RMs affect that change hinges on their day-to-day activities. RMs who exert positive influences are those who tend to be more effective, those whose activities are especially related to communication and human resource management. However, RMs who are *not* effective also shape the organizational culture. When they are deliberately destructive and counterproductive, they shape it negatively. Fortunately, most organizations are resilient—they bounce back and not only survive, but can still thrive. In good economic conditions, organizations survive in spite of, rather than because of, the way they are managed. In tight economic times, and especially in an era of intense global competition, American organizations will have to devote more attention to the positive, effective activities of RMs that shape organizational culture.

As it turns out, the equation for Real Managers is not that complicated. Being successful and effective means accomplishing your day-to-day activities better than you have before; it doesn't mean unlocking some innovative or secret method. In our study, we were most impressed by the awakened spirit among RMs to do better, to become excellent. For too long, the formulas for achieving managerial excellence, at least in modern America, have focused on technology and such functional skills as marketing, finance, and production.

Our study of RMs suggests that it is much simpler than that. We found that RMs do the things we have known about for decades—traditional management and communication. But they are also doing more: human resource management and networking activities. It is the latter two overlooked sets of activities and their relationships that are the key to managerial excellence. Resolving, if not eliminating, the difference between successful and effective Real Managers may be the key challenge for true managerial excellence in the critical years ahead.

Supplemental Readings and Original References

The text of *Real Managers* contains no specific references or footnotes because, except in a the few cases noted, it presents original data. We also wanted to keep it as readable as possible. There are, nevertheless, a number of relevant background as well as directly relevant references for the interested reader. The foundation for our study comes primarily from social learning theory. The most comprehensive and widely recognized source for social learning theory can be found in Albert Bandura, *Social Learning Theory*, (Englewood Cliffs, N.J.: Prentice-Hall, 1977).

More specific application of social learning and observational techniques to leadership and managerial behavior can be found in Fred Luthans, "Leadership: A Proposal for Social Learning Theory Base and Observational and Functional Analysis Techniques to Measure Leader Behavior," in *Crosscurrents in Leadership*, ed. James G. Hunt and Lars L. Larson (Carbondale: Southern Illinois University Press, 1979), pp. 201-208.

Luthans and Tim R.V. Davis published a number of articles giving further details on social learning approach. These were used as the point of departure and perspective for the present study. None of them, however, contained data from the present study. These include the following:

Tim R.V. Davis and Fred Luthans, "Leadership Re-Examined: A Behavioral Approach," *Academy of Management Review* 4, no. 2 (June 1979): 237-48.

Fred Luthans and Tim R.V. Davis, "Behavioral Self-Management: The Missing Link in Managerial Effectiveness," *Organizational Dynamics* 18, no. 1 (Summer 1979): 42-60.

Tim R.V. Davis and Fred Luthans, "Managers in Action: A New Look at their Behavior and Operating Modes," *Organizational Dynamics* 9, no. 1 (Summer 1980): 64-80

Tim R.V. Davis and Fred Luthans, "A Social Learning Approach to Organizational Behavior," *Academy of Management Review* 5, no. 2 (June 1980): 281-90.

Fred Luthans and Tim R.V. Davis, "Beyond Modeling: Managing Social Learning Processes in Human Resource Training and Development," *Human Resource Management* (Summer 1981): 19-27.

Tim R.V. Davis and Fred Luthans, "Defining and Researching Leadership as a Behavioral Construct: An Idiographic Approach," *Journal of Applied Behavioral Science* 20, no. 3 (August 1984): 237-51.

Luthans and Robert Kreitner also used social learning theory to expand the operant learning approach to what they call organizational behavior modification, or O.B. Mod. The following works expand on the O.B. Mod. Approach, which also is used as a point of departure and perspective, but no data, for *Real Managers:*

Robert Kreitner and Fred Luthans, "A Social Learning approach to Behavioral Management: Radical Behaviorists 'Mellowing' Out," *Organizational Dynamics* 13, no. 2 (Autumn 1984): 61-75.

Fred Luthans and Robert Kreitner, *Organizational Behavior Modification and Beyond* (Glenview Ill.: Scott Foresman, 1985).

In addition to the theoretical foundation and perspectives provided by the above references, the present study drew from the following methodological perspectives provided in articles by Luthans and Davis and Luthans and Nancy Morey:

Fred Luthans and Tim R.V. Davis, "An Idiographic Approach to Organizational Behavior Research: The Use of Single Case Experimental Designs and Direct Measures," *Academy of Management Review* 7, no. 3 (July 1982): 380-91.

Nancy Morey and Fred Luthans; "An Emic Perspective and Ethno-Science Methods for Organizational Research," *Academy of Management Review* 9, no. 1 (January 1984): 27-36.

Nancy Morey and Fred Luthans, "Refining the Displacement of Culture and Use of Scenes and Themes in Organizational Studies," *Academy of Management Review* 10, no. 2 (April 1985): 219-29.

The three standardized questionnaires used in the effectiveness analysis reported in Chapter 4 were drawn from:

Paul E. Mott, *The Characteristics of Effective Organizations* (New York, Harper & Rowe, 1972). (This book contains the questionnaire for organizational effectiveness in terms of the quantity and quality of performance of the work unit.)

Richard T. Mowday, L.W. Porter, and Richard M. Steers, *Employee-Organizational Linkages: The Psychology of Commitment, Absenteeism, and Turnover* (New York: Academic Press 1982). (This book contains the Organizational Commitment Questionnaire.)

P.C. Smith, L.M. Kendall, and C.L. Hulin, *The Measurement of Satisfaction in Work and Retirement* (Chicago, Rand-McNally, 1969). (This contains the Job Diagnostic Index that measures employee satisfaction.)

The following article by Luthans and Diane Lockwood is the most directly related reference to *Real Managers* that describes in detail the derivation of the managerial activities and the reliability and validity analyses:

Fred Luthans and Diane Lockwood, "Toward an Observation System for Measuring Leader Behavior in Natural Settings," in *Leaders and Managers: International Perspectives of Managerial Behavior and Leadership*, eds. J. Hunt, D. Hosking, C. Schreischeim, and R. Stewart (New York: Pergamon Press, 1984), 117-41.

The data base for Real Managers generated two specialized articles:

Fred Luthans, Stuart Rosenkrantz, and Harry Hennessey, "What do Successful Managers Really Do? An Observational Study of Managerial Activities;" *Journal of Applied Behavioral Science* 21, no. 3 (August 1985): 255-70.

Fred Luthans and Janet K. Larsen, "How Managers Really Communicate," *Human Relations* 39, no. 2 (February 1986): 161-78.

There are other articles that draw from the *Real Managers* data base. The interested reader will find details of the samples used, measurement techniques, and statistical analysis in the above articles, especially in the Luthans and Lockwood article.

Besides the above directly related references to the study of *Real Managers*, the text discussion mentioned other authors. Here is a full reference list for the interested reader:

Bass, Bernard M. *Leadership and Performance Beyond Expectations.* New York: Free Press, 1985.

Bolman, L.G. and T.E. Deal. *Modern Approaches to Understanding and Managing Organizations.* San Francisco: Jossey Bass, 1984.

Culbert, S.A. and J.J. McDonough. *Radical Management.* New York: Free Press, 1985.

Fayol, Henri. *General and Industrial Management.* Translated by Constance Storrs. London: Pittman, 1949.

Gulick, Luther. "Notes on the Theory of Organization." In *Papers on the Science of Administration,* edited by Luther Gulick and Lyndall Urwick. New York: Institute of Public Administration, 1937.

Koontz, Harold. "The Management Theory Jungle." *Academy of Management Journal* 4, no. 3 (December 1961): 174-88.

—————. "The Management Theory Jungle Revisited." *Academy of Management Review* 5, no. 2 (April 1980): 175-87.

—————. "What Effective General Managers Really Do." *Harvard Business Review* 60, no. 6 (November-December 1982): 156-67.

Likert, Rensis. *The Human Organization.* New York: McGraw-Hill, 1967.

McClelland, David C. *The Achieving Society.* Princeton, N.J.: Van Norstrand, 1961.

—————. "The Two Faces of Power." *Journal of International Affairs* 24, no. 1 (1970): pp. 29-47.

Mintzberg, Henry. *The Nature of Managerial Work.* New York: Harper & Row, 1973.

—————. "The Manager's Job: Folklore and Fact." *Harvard Business Review* 53, no. 4 (July-August 1975): 49-61.

Peters, Thomas J. and Robert H. Waterman, Jr. *In Search of Excellence: Lessons from America's Best-Run Companies.* New York: Harper & Row, 1982.

Urwick, Lyndall. *The Elements of Administration.* New York: Harper, 1943.

About the Author

FRED LUTHANS is a three-time graduate of the University of Iowa (BA in Math, 1961; MBA, 1962; PhD in Management/Psychology, 1965). After 2-years active duty as a Captain in the U.S. Army teaching Psychology and Leadership at West Point, his 50-year academic career has been at Nebraska where he is University and George Holmes Distinguished Professor of Management, Emeritus. A former President of the Academy of Management, he also received the Academy's Distinguished Educator Award, Publications Hall of Fame, Lifetime Achievement Award and is a Fellow of AOM, DSI, and PPBA. He also received the University of Iowa Distinguished Alumni Award, an Honorary Doctorate from De Paul, Harvard Medical School's Award for Leadership in Behavioral Health and Clinton High School Alumni Hall of Fame. Luthans has edited three top journals and authored several well-known books and over 250 academic articles and chapters. In total, his work currently has over 72,000 citations and his H-Index is 100 and i-10 is 224. Last year he was named to Web of Science's Top 1% Citations for all researchers in the world and this year was ranked in top 1% Citations in all of Business and Economics, 10th in H-Factor, and #1 cited in Organizational Behavior texts. Professor Luthans's research at first focused on what he termed O.B. Mod. (organizational behavior modification) and successful and effective managerial behavior (Real Managers). More recently, he has consulted with numerous high-profile organizations and focused on the theory-building, measurement, research and application of what he founded and has termed "positive organizational behavior (POB)" and "psychological capital (PsyCap)", a multi-dimensional core construct consisting of the positive psychological resources of hope, efficacy (confidence), resilience, and optimism or the HERO Within. Over the years, he has lectured in most countries in the world.

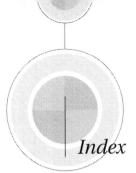

Index

Made in the USA
Monee, IL
13 May 2023

33585989R00120